FOREIGN AFFAIRS

Special Collection

FIGHTING

Foreign Affairs iPad Extra: Endgame in Iraq

Editor Gideon Rose Introduces the Collection

Ever since the Bush administration invaded Iraq, the question of what role the United States should play in Iraq's destiny has been open and hotly debated. Some policymakers wanted to get out as quickly as possible. Others felt it was important to remain. From 2003–6, the United States had its eye on the exits. But then, with the surge, it decided to stay. It left in 2009, and now the consequences of that decision are unfolding. We at *Foreign Affairs* are happy to offer this collection to put breaking events into context.

ON THE RUN-UP TO WAR:
Kenneth Pollack, a senior fellow at the Brookings Institution, writes in 2002 that, after the war in Afghanistan, the Bush administration should turn to Iraq.

ON THE SURGE:
Steven Simon, a senior fellow at the Middle East Institute, explains in 2008 why the surge won't leave a stable Iraq.

ON SECTARIANISM:
Iraq experts Emma Sky and Harith al-Qarawee document the rise in 2013 of militant Sunni groups calling for an Iraqi Sunnistan.

ON ISIS:
Barak Mendelsohn, an associate professor of political science, describes in 2014 how ISIS could supplant al Qaeda as the jihadi movement's most powerful group.

Visit ForeignAffairs.com for more on these topics—and all our other great content.

Iraq's Descent

Chronicle of a Death Foretold

Gideon Rose

Ever since the Bush administration invaded Iraq in 2003, the question of what would follow Saddam Hussein's regime—and what role the United States would play in Iraq's ultimate destiny—has been open and hotly debated.

Some policymakers wanted to get out as quickly as possible, essentially leaving Iraq to its own devices. Others felt it was important to stay for the longer term, helping to provide for Iraqi security and trying to guide the new Iraqi state on a healthy path.

From 2003 to 2006, the Bush administration essentially kept one eye on the exits. Then, as Iraq descended into civil war, it shifted course, adopting a new policy, the surge, and taking a greater and more open-ended role in maintaining order.

As the civil war subsided and relative calm returned to Iraq, the Bush administration negotiated an agreement for U.S. forces to leave the country. The Obama administration accepted and implemented it to the letter, happy to put the conflict squarely in the rear-view mirror.

Now, the ultimate consequences of that decision are playing themselves out. Without much American involvement or tutelage, Iraq is once again descending into civil war. The Maliki government has governed poorly and alienated much of Iraq's non-Shia population. ISIS, a Sunni extremist group that started out in eastern Syria, has spread to western Iraq and has declared a new caliphate, or Islamic state, in heavily Sunni parts of both countries. The Kurds in northeastern Iraq are operating largely on their own. And

GIDEON ROSE is Editor of *Foreign Affairs*.

what role the United States should play in Iraq is once again at the forefront of the American foreign policy agenda.

At *Foreign Affairs*, we've been tracking these decisions in real time, featuring a broad range of expert perspectives from across the political spectrum. As the fate of Iraq appears to hang in the balance once again, we offer this collection to put breaking events in their proper intellectual and historical context.

Next Stop Baghdad?

Kenneth M. Pollack

CUTTING THE GORDIAN KNOT

As the conflict in Afghanistan winds down, the question of what the United States should do about Iraq has risen to the forefront of American foreign policy. Hawks argue that toppling Saddam Hussein should be "phase two" in the war on terrorism. They see Iraq's development of unconventional weapons as a critical threat to U.S. national interests and want to parlay the success of the Afghan campaign into a similar operation further west. Those who pass for doves in the mainstream debate point to the difficulty of such an undertaking and the lack of any evidence tying Saddam to the recent attacks on the United States. They argue that the goal of America's Iraq policy should be to revive U.N. weapons inspections and re-energize containment. Both camps have it partly right—and partly wrong.

Thanks to Washington's own missed opportunities and others' shameful cynicism, there are no longer any good policy options toward Iraq. The hawks are wrong to think the problem is desperately urgent or connected to terrorism, but they are right to see the prospect of a nuclear-armed Saddam as so worrisome that it requires drastic action. The doves, meanwhile, are right about Iraq's not being a good candidate for a replay of Operation Enduring Freedom, but they are wrong to think that inspections and deterrence are adequate responses to Iraq's weapons of mass destruction (WMD) programs.

After the more immediate danger posed by Osama bin Laden's al Qaeda network has been dealt with, the Bush administration

Kenneth M. Pollack is Senior Fellow and Deputy Director for National Security Studies at the Council on Foreign Relations. From 1999 to 2001 he served as Director for Gulf Affairs on the staff of the National Security Council.

should indeed turn its attention to Baghdad. What it should do at that point, however, is pursue the one strategy that offers a way out of the impasse. The United States should invade Iraq, eliminate the present regime, and pave the way for a successor prepared to abide by its international commitments and live in peace with its neighbors.

THE TROUBLE WITH CONTAINMENT

The reasons for contemplating such dramatic action have little to do with the events of September 11 and the subsequent crisis and much to do with the course of U.S. policy toward Iraq since 1991. After Iraq's defeat in the Persian Gulf War, the first Bush administration hoped Saddam would fall from power. It had no clear strategy for how to make that happen, however, and so settled for keeping him isolated and defanged until the lucky day eventually arrived. For lack of a better alternative the Clinton administration continued the same policy, as has the current administration.

The central goal of containment over the past decade has been to prevent Saddam—a serial aggressor—from rebuilding Iraq's military power, including its weapons of mass destruction. The United States and its allies did not want to have to deter, repel, or reverse another Iraqi invasion; they wanted to deny Saddam the wherewithal to mount a threat to his neighbors in the first place. So they put in place, under U.N. auspices, a combination of economic, military, and diplomatic constraints that prevented Saddam from once again destabilizing one of the world's most strategically important regions, while simultaneously allowing humanitarian exemptions so Iraq could meet the nonmilitary needs of its population. Despite the criticism it often received, this policy was a sensible approach to a situation in which there were few attractive options. It served its purposes well, and far longer than most thought possible.

Over the last few years, however, containment has started to unravel. Serious inspections of Saddam's WMD programs stopped long ago. Fewer and fewer nations respect the U.N.-mandated constraints, and more and more are tired of constantly battling with Saddam to force him to comply. Ludicrous Iraqi propaganda about how the economic sanctions are responsible for the deaths of more than a million people since 1991 is now accepted at face value the world over. A dozen or more nations have flown commercial airliners into Iraq to flout the ban on air travel to and from the country—a ban they now claim never existed, but one that was a well-respected fact just a few years ago. Smuggled Iraqi oil flows via Jordan, Syria, Turkey, and the Persian Gulf states at a rate more than double what it was in 1998. Iraq is increasingly able to get its hands on prohibited items such as spare parts for its tanks and planes and equipment for its crippled logistical system. Most stunning of all, the Chinese were recently caught building a nationwide fiber-optic communications network for Saddam's regime; the key nodes of this system were destroyed by U.S. airstrikes in January 2001. If respect for the sanctions has already eroded to the point where the Chinese are willing to sell Iraq such critical technology, how long will it be before someone proves willing to sell tanks? Or missiles? Or fissile material?

Repeated calls to resuscitate the anti-Saddam coalition and strengthen containment are correct about the problem but naïve in thinking it can be solved easily. Comprehensive sanctions of the type imposed on Iraq are of necessity a multilateral effort, and at this point there are simply too many important countries willing to subvert them for the scheme to be effective. The current administration's unhappy experience in trying to sell "smart sanctions" to the international community shows just how bad the situation is. The administration's proposed reforms would lift most of the economic constraints on Iraq in return for tighter controls over what comes into the country—a perfectly reasonable idea for anyone actually interested in helping the Iraqi people while keeping Saddam's military in check. But France, Russia, China, and others have opposed the plan because Baghdad fears, correctly, that if it were accepted some form of international military and financial controls might be prolonged.

Ironically, in practice the smart sanctions probably would not do much more than briefly stave off containment's collapse. Right now the U.N. uses its control over Iraq's contracts to determine what goes into and out of the country legally. The system is policed through U.N. (read U.S.) scrutiny of every Iraqi contract—a cumbersome and glacially slow process that still fails to stop Saddam's massive smuggling activities. The Bush administration's proposal would shift the enforcement burden away from the U.N. and onto Iraq's neighbors and try to shut down illegal trade by buying the cooperation of those states through which it would have to pass— Jordan, Syria, Turkey, Iran, and the members of the Gulf Cooperation Council (Bahrain, Kuwait, Oman, Qatar, Saudi Arabia, and the United Arab Emirates). The problem is that all these countries profit from the smuggling, all have populations opposed to enforcing the sanctions, and all except the GCC and Iran are now highly vulnerable to Iraqi economic pressure. So no matter what they may say publicly, none of them is likely to help much in blocking the flow of oil, money, and contraband.

At this point, restoring a serious and sustainable containment regime would require an entirely new set of arrangements. General economic sanctions would have to be lifted and the current U.N. contracting system virtually eliminated, while the core military embargo and financial controls would have to be left in place, harsh penalties instituted for violators, and preauthorization arranged for the use of force by the United States to compel compliance. Such a deal is unimaginable in the U.N. Security Council today, where many of the members compete to see who can appease Iraq most. And although in theory similar reforms could be imposed by the United States unilaterally, any attempt to do so would soon run into passionate international opposition, crippling U.S. diplomacy long before it had much effect on Saddam. Reforming containment enough to make it viable, therefore, is simply not in the offing.

THE TROUBLE WITH DETERRENCE

In response to the problems of containment, some have argued that the United States should fall back on a strategy of deterrence—or rather, containment as it was actually practiced against the Soviet Union during the Cold War (as opposed to the supersized version applied to Iraq in the 1990s). This would mean allowing the post-Gulf War constraints to slip away altogether and relying solely on the threat of U.S. intervention to dissuade Saddam from future aggression. Such an approach would be generally welcome outside the United States. But it would involve running a terrible risk, for it is not at all clear that Saddam can be deterred successfully for very long.

This is not to argue that Saddam is irrational. There is considerable evidence that he weighs costs and benefits, follows a crude logic in determining how best to achieve his goals, understands deterrence, and has been deterred in the past. Few knowledgeable observers doubt that Saddam refrained from using WMD when he attacked Israel during the Gulf War because he feared Israeli nuclear retaliation, and he seems to have been deterred from using WMD against Saudi Arabia and coalition forces because he feared U.S. retaliation.

Nevertheless, Saddam has a number of pathologies that make deterring him unusually difficult. He is an inveterate gambler and risk-taker who regularly twists his calculation of the odds to suit his preferred course of action. He bases his calculations on assumptions that outsiders often find bizarre and has little understanding of the larger world. He is a solitary decision-maker who relies little on advice from others. And he has poor sources of information about matters outside Iraq, along with intelligence services that generally tell him what they believe he wants to hear. These pathologies lie behind the many terrible miscalculations Saddam has made over the years that flew in the face of deterrence—including the invasion of Iran in 1980, the invasion of Kuwait in 1990, the decision to fight for Kuwait in 1990-91, and the decision to threaten Kuwait again in 1994.

It is thus impossible to predict the kind of calculations he would make about the willingness of the United States to challenge him once he had the ability to incinerate Riyadh, Tel Aviv, or the Saudi oil fields. He might well make another grab for Kuwait, for example, and once in possession dare the United States to evict him and risk a nuclear exchange. During the Cold War, U.S. strategists used to fret that once the Soviet Union reached strategic parity, Moscow would feel free to employ its conventional forces as it saw fit because the United States would be too scared of escalation to respond. Such fears were plausible in the abstract but seem to have been groundless because Soviet leaders were fundamentally conservative decision-makers. Saddam, in contrast, is fundamentally aggressive and risk-acceptant. Leaving him free to acquire nuclear weapons and then hoping that in spite of his track record he can be deterred this time around is not the kind of social science experiment the United States government should be willing to run.

PHASE TWO?

With containment collapsing and deterrence too risky, some form of regime change is steadily becoming the only answer to the Iraqi conundrum. In the wake of the September 11 attacks, in fact, supporters of one particular approach to regime change—using the Iraqi opposition to do the job, in conjunction with U.S. air power— have repackaged their ideas to fit the times and gained substantial momentum. The position of these hawks was captured succinctly in a September 20 "open letter" to President Bush from three dozen luminaries, who argued that any strategy aiming at the eradication of terrorism and its sponsors must include a determined effort to remove Saddam Hussein from power in Iraq. Failure to undertake such an effort will constitute an early and perhaps decisive surrender in the war on international terrorism. The United States must therefore provide full military and financial support to the Iraqi opposition. American military force should be used to provide a "safe zone" in Iraq from which the opposition can operate. Once the military operations in Afghanistan succeeded, they were widely touted by such hawks as a model for a future campaign against Saddam.

The hawks are right on two big points: that a nuclear-armed Saddam would be a disaster waiting to happen and that at this point it would be easier to get rid of him than to stop him from reconstituting his weapons programs. Unfortunately, most of them are wrong on key details, such as how regime change should be accomplished. Trying to topple Saddam by using the same limited military approach the United States used in Afghanistan—air power, special forces, and support for local opposition groups—would be trying to do the job on the cheap, and like all such efforts would run a real risk of disaster. It is possible that the Afghan strategy would work against Iraq—but not likely.

In recent wars, U.S. air power has repeatedly proven devastating, and against Iraq it could by itself undoubtedly accomplish numerous missions. A determined air campaign that focused on Saddam's key supporters—the Republican Guard, the Special Republican Guard, the Baath Party, the Saddam Fedayeen, and the internal security services—might spark a coup. Indeed, in December 1998 Operation Desert Fox struck at this target set and Saddam became so concerned about a coup that he overreacted, ordering emergency security measures, including the arrest and assassination of several important Shi`ite clerics, that set off uprisings among Iraq's Shi`a communities. If the intention is to coerce Saddam into respecting U.N. sanctions or modest U.S. dictates, then an open-ended air campaign along the lines of Desert Fox would likely do the trick.

But coercing Saddam by threatening his overthrow is one thing, and making sure that overthrow occurs is another. The fact is that Desert Fox did not produce a coup, and the unrest that Saddam created through his overreaction was easily suppressed. All available evidence indicates that even an Afghan-style war effort would have little chance of eliminating the regime in Iraq, because of the many differences between the two cases.

In Afghanistan, the military balance between the opposition and the Taliban was quite close, which is why limited U.S. actions were able to tip the scales decisively. The Northern Alliance fighters had frustrated the much larger and better-armed Taliban forces on the battlefield for seven years. Although the Taliban slowly gained control over most of the country, the Northern Alliance always gave ground grudgingly, making the Taliban pay for every step. In Iraq, in contrast, the gap in capabilities between the regime and the opposition is much wider. In 1991 and again in 1996, Saddam's Republican Guard easily defeated even the strongest of the local Iraqi opposition forces, the two Kurdish militias. If the United States were to provide the Kurds with weapons, training, funds, and massive air support, at some point they would probably be able to hold their territory against an Iraqi assault—but even then they would have great difficulty translating such a defensive capability into the offensive power needed to overthrow Saddam.

Some argue that with U.S. aid the external Iraqi opposition, principally the Iraq National Congress (INC), could play the Northern Alliance role. But the INC has several big strikes against it. None of Iraq's neighbors is willing to serve as a sanctuary for it because they consider it ineffectual. The INC lacks competent field commanders and has never demonstrated any serious support inside Iraq. Even with U.S. help and a base of operations in northern Iraq from 1992 to 1996, it could never gather more than a few hundred fighters at a time, was heavily reliant on the Kurds for military operations, and was unable to secure any significant defections from the Iraqi armed forces.

If the Iraqi opposition is much weaker than the Northern Alliance, the Iraqi regime is also much stronger than the Taliban was. The Taliban fielded perhaps 45,000 troops, while Iraq has armed forces totaling 400,000—one-quarter of them in the elite Republican Guard and Special Republican Guard—along with paramilitary forces totaling hundreds of thousands more. The Iraqi army is much better armed than the Taliban was, has better discipline, and has demonstrated better unit cohesion. The Iraqi armed forces are hardly a juggernaut, but they have repeatedly proved to be more than a match for all local opposition.

Saddam's control over Iraq, meanwhile, is much stronger than the Taliban's control was over Afghanistan. He has quashed countless coup attempts, insurrections, and even outright revolts during his decades in power, and this has made the average Iraqi very wary of taking action of any kind against his regime. It is true that following Saddam's catastrophic defeat in the Gulf War there were major rebellions throughout southern Iraq. But what is noteworthy about them is not how large they were, but how small. Despite the magnitude of Saddam's defeat, only several tens of thousands of people ever joined in the uprisings. Despite their passionate hatred of Saddam, the vast majority of Iraqis were so terrified of him that they chose to wait to see how things would turn out rather than join the rebellion and risk retribution if it failed.

WOULD THIS TIME BE DIFFERENT?

The key to victory in Afghanistan was a U.S. air campaign that routed the Taliban combat forces, leaving the Northern Alliance only the tasks of reducing several isolated strongholds and generally mopping up. In Iraq, U.S. air power would have to accomplish at least the same results for an Afghan-style strategy to succeed, but on this score history is not encouraging.

In Operation Desert Storm, the United States hit Iraq with what was probably the most powerful preliminary air campaign in history. It followed this up with one of the most decisive ground campaigns of the twentieth century. By early March 1991, the Iraqi armed forces had been reduced to a shadow of their former selves. Yet weak as they were, they still had enough strength to crush the largest insurrections in Iraqi history and keep Saddam in power. Those who favor the Afghan approach against Iraq are therefore betting that a U.S. military effort significantly smaller than the one mounted in 1991 would somehow produce much greater results this time around.

Some claim that U.S. and Iraqi forces today are so different from those a decade ago that such history is no longer relevant. Iraq's military is certainly not as capable as it once was. And since 1991, improvements in command, control, communications, and intelligence capabilities, together with the greater availability and effectiveness of precision-guided munitions, have made the U.S. military machine far more deadly. In one crucial area, however—the ability to break enemy ground forces using air strikes alone—the vast strides the U.S. military has taken since 1991 have yielded only a modest improvement.

Most of the U.S. advances have come in using fewer forces to destroy a given target. But throughout history the key determinant of whether ground units are likely to collapse from air strikes alone has not been the accuracy of the blows, but rather the commitment and discipline of the troops being struck. This point was reinforced in Afghanistan, where the less committed Taliban troops broke under U.S. airstrikes but the more determined and disciplined al Qaeda units did not—and fought hard later at Kunduz, Kandahar, and Tora Bora.

The same was true during the Gulf War, when Iraq's low-grade infantry divisions broke under the massive U.S. air campaign, but the more determined and disciplined Republican Guard and regular army heavy divisions did not. This was hardly for lack of trying. The coalition flew 110,000 sorties against Iraq during Desert Storm, compared to only 6,500 against the Taliban by the fall of Kandahar. It hit the key Republican Guard divisions with more than 1,000 sorties apiece, used twice as many precision- guided munitions against Iraq as against the Taliban, and destroyed perhaps 1,500 Iraqi armored fighting vehicles from the air. The United States waged a far more punishing air campaign against Iraq than it did against the Taliban, in other words, and inflicted far more damage on Iraqi forces. But the key Iraqi divisions never broke and fought hard, although not particularly well, during the coalition's subsequent ground offensive. The odds are, therefore, that even today a substantial part of Saddam's forces would weather a sustained aerial attack, and even badly battered would still be able to prevail in combat against the opposition afterward.

Using the Afghan approach in Iraq, moreover, would leave the United States dangerously vulnerable to Saddam's counterattacks. Once Saddam realized that Washington was serious about regime change, he would fight back with everything he had—including the two or three dozen Scud-type missiles with biological and chemical warheads that U.N. inspectors and U.S. intelligence believe he has stashed away. During the Gulf War, the United States was unable to find Iraq's Scud launchers in the western and southern parts of the country even though it used large numbers of aircraft and special forces teams in the effort. American capabilities have improved since then, but few in the U.S. military have confidence that the same mix of forces would do much better today. Likewise, once an Afghan-style air campaign began, Saddam would have every incentive to crush the Kurds. Since America's ability to defend them without ground forces is extremely limited, it has relied on deterrence—the threat of a massive air campaign—instead. If such an air campaign is going on anyway, that threat will no longer work, and Saddam would likely move to reoccupy the north—with all of the attendant slaughter and repression that would entail.

Saddam might also decide to shut down Iraqi oil production to try to force Washington to halt its attacks. The U.S. strategic petroleum reserve could compensate for the loss of Iraqi oil for about seven months, but the uncertain length of an Afghan-style campaign against Iraq would raise the possibility that U.S. reserves might run out before Saddam fell. Unless U.S. ground forces occupied the Iraqi oil fields at the start of a war, moreover, there would be little to prevent Saddam from destroying them as a final act of vengeance, just as he destroyed Kuwait's oil fields in 1991.

Carrying off an Afghan-style campaign against Iraq, finally, would be extremely difficult without the support of a number of regional partners—to provide bases and overflight for the air campaign, conduits and safe havens for the opposition forces, help with making up any shortfalls in Iraqi oil production, and so forth.

Indeed, the Afghan operations themselves required help from countries including Pakistan, Uzbekistan, Kyrgyzstan, Tajikistan, Russia, and India. A replay against Iraq, a much larger and harder target, would require a comparable lineup of local friends.

Unfortunately, this is the one approach to the problem that the frontline states have made clear they would not support. America's allies in the region have told Washington time and again that they will not assist any U.S. military operation with an indeterminate end and low chances of success. As one high-ranking GCC official has put it, "when you are ready to use all of your forces we will be there for you, but we're not interested in letting you try out theories about air power."

THE CASE FOR INVASION

Saddam Hussein must be dealt with. But thinking about Iraq in the context of the war on terrorism or the operations in Afghanistan obscures more than it clarifies. Given the specific features of the Iraqi situation, trying to topple Saddam with an Afghan-style campaign would be risky and ill advised. It might just work, but there is no reason to chance it, especially since adding a major ground component—that is, replaying the Gulf War rather than the Afghan campaign—would not cost much more while making success a near certainty. Even without committing its own ground forces, the United States would still be responsible for Iraq's political and military reconstruction. Using a standoff approach to regime change, however, would limit American ability to control events while opening the door to mischief-makers who would try to turn Saddam's fall to their own advantage. Because of the human, diplomatic, and financial costs involved, invasion should always be a last resort. Unfortunately in this case, since all the other options are worse, it is a necessary one.

The strategic logic for invasion is compelling. It would eliminate the possibility that Saddam might rebuild his military or acquire nuclear weapons and thus threaten the security of the world's supply of oil. It would allow the United States to redeploy most of its forces away from the region afterward, or at the very least return to its pre-Gulf War "over the horizon" presence—something long sought by locals and the United States alike. And by facilitating the reconstruction of Iraq and its re-entry into regional politics it would remove a major irritant from U.S. relations with the Muslim world in general.

The military aspects of an invasion, meanwhile, although hardly painless, would be straightforward and well within U.S. capabilities. In 1991, U.S. forces ran roughshod over their Iraqi counterparts, and in the ten years since then the gap in capabilities between the two sides has widened. At this point, the United States could probably smash Iraq's ground forces with a single corps composed of two heavy divisions and an armored cavalry regiment. To be on the safe side and to handle other missions, however, it would make sense to plan for a force twice that size. Some light infantry will be required in case Saddam's loyalists fight in Iraq's cities. Airmobile forces will be needed to seize Iraq's oil fields at the start of hostilities and to occupy the sites from which Saddam could launch missiles against Israel or Saudi Arabia. And troops will have to be available for occupation duties once the fighting is over. All told, the force should total roughly 200,000-300,000 people: for the invasion, between four and six divisions plus supporting units, and for the air campaign, 700-1,000 aircraft and anywhere from one to five carrier battle groups (depending on what sort of access to bases turned out to be possible). Building up such a force in the Persian Gulf would take three to five months, but the campaign itself would probably take about a month, including the opening air operations.

The casualties incurred during such an operation might well be greater than during the Afghan or Gulf Wars, but they are unlikely to be catastrophic. Two factors that could increase the toll would be the willingness of Iraqi forces to fight tenaciously for their cities and a decision by Saddam to employ unconventional weapons during the crisis. On the other hand, it is possible that the mere presence of such American forces on Iraq's doorstep could produce a coup that would topple Saddam without significant combat.

The military aspects of an invasion, actually, are likely to be the easiest part of the deal. The diplomatic fallout will probably be more difficult, with its severity directly related to the length of the campaign and the certainty of its outcome. Just as in Afghanistan, the longer it drags on and the more uncertain it looks, the more dissent will be heard, both at home and abroad—whereas the quicker and more decisive the victory, the more palatable it will be for all concerned.

The only country whose support would be absolutely necessary for an invasion is Kuwait. The task would be made dramatically easier if the Saudis helped, however, both because of the excellent bases on their territory and because the GCC and Jordan would undoubtedly follow the Saudi lead. Although both the Saudis and the Kuwaitis have said they do not want the United States to attack Iraq, the consensus among those who know those countries' leaders well is that they would grudgingly consent if the United States could convince them it was willing to use the full range of its military capabilities to ensure a swift, successful campaign.

Egyptian permission would be required to move ships through the Suez Canal and planes across its airspace, but given the importance of U.S. economic and military assistance to Egypt that should not be a problem. Turkey's support would also be useful, in particular because it would make it much easier to defend the Kurds in northern Iraq from an Iraqi counteroffensive. Other regional states would have an incentive to come on board because they would want to have a say in the postinvasion political arrangements in Baghdad. The French, the Russians, and the Chinese would object strongly to the whole concept and might try to kill it by raising a diplomatic firestorm. Still, they could not stop a U.S. invasion were the administration truly set on one, and they might eventually jump on board once it went ahead if only to retain political and economic influence in Iraq later on.

The biggest headaches for the United States are likely to stem not from the invasion itself but from its aftermath. Once the country has been conquered and Saddam's regime driven from power, the United States would be left "owning" a country of 22 million people ravaged by more than two decades of war, totalitarian misrule, and severe deprivation. The invaders would get to decide the composition and form of a future Iraqi government—both an opportunity and a burden. Some form of unitary but federalized state would probably best suit the bewildering array of local and foreign interests involved, but ideally this decision would be a collective one: as in Afghanistan, the United States should try to turn the question of future Iraqi political arrangements over to the U.N., or possibly the Arab League, thus shedding and spreading some responsibility for the outcome. Alternatively, it might bring in those countries most directly affected by the outcome—the Saudis, Kuwaitis, Jordanians, and Turks—both to co-opt them and as an incentive for their diplomatic support. In the end, of course, it would be up to the United States to make sure that a post-Saddam Iraq did not slip into chaos like Lebanon in the 1980s or Afghanistan in the 1990s, creating spillover effects in the region and raising the possibility of a new terrorist haven.

Because it will be important to ensure that Iraq does not fall apart afterward, the United States will also need to repair much of the damage done to the Iraqi economy since Saddam's accession. It could undoubtedly raise substantial funds for this purpose from the GCC and perhaps some European and East Asian allies dependent on Persian Gulf oil. And as soon as Iraq's oil started flowing again, the country could contribute to its own future. Current estimates of the cost of rebuilding Iraq's economy, however, range from $50 billion to $150 billion, and that does not include repairing the damage from yet another major war. The United States should thus be prepared to contribute several billion dollars per year for as much as a decade to rebuild the country.

IF NOT NOW, WHEN?

It is one thing to recognize that because of the unique features of this case—the scale of the interests involved, Saddam's unparalleled record of aggression and violence, and the problems with other options—an invasion of Iraq is the least bad course of action available. It is another to figure out just when such an invasion should be launched. Despite what many hawks now argue, it is a mistake to think of operations against Iraq as part of the war on terrorism. The dilemma the United States must now grapple with, in fact, is that attacking Iraq could jeopardize the success of that war, but the longer it waits before attacking the harder it will be and the greater the risk that Saddam's strength will increase.

Toppling Saddam is not a necessary component of the war on terrorism, and by itself Iraq's support for terrorism would not justify the heavy costs of an invasion. Iraq is indeed a state sponsor of terrorism, but on the grand roll of such sponsors it is well behind Iran, Syria, Pakistan, Sudan, Lebanon, North Korea, Libya, and several others. If the only problem the United States had with Iraq were its support for terrorism, it would be a relatively minor concern. Conversely, if one were to list Saddam Hussein's crimes against humanity in order of their importance, his support for terrorism would rank low.

The reason for even contemplating all the costs that an invasion would entail is the risk that a nuclear-armed Saddam might wreak havoc in his region and beyond, together with the certainty that he will acquire such weapons eventually if left unchecked. Nevertheless, there is no indication that he is about to get them within weeks or months. Containment may be dying, but it is not dead yet, and a determined U.S. effort could keep it alive for some time longer. Iraq represents an emerging threat, but bin Laden and his accomplices constitute an immediate one.

Al Qaeda has demonstrated both the ability and the willingness to reach into the American homeland and slaughter thousands, and it now has the motive of revenge to add to its general ideological hostility. Breaking the network's back in Afghanistan and elsewhere should therefore be the Bush administration's top national security priority, and this cannot be done without the active cooperation of scores of U.S. allies around the world—for intelligence gathering, police work, and financial cooperation, all on top of any military or diplomatic help that might be required.

So far the administration's efforts in this area are paying off, largely because others have supported them. Should that trend continue, it is likely that within anywhere from six months to two years the United States and its partners will have disrupted al Qaeda's communications, recruitment, financing, and planning so much that what is left of the network will be largely innocuous. Until this point has been reached, it would be a mistake to jeopardize success by risking a major break with U.S. allies—something that a serious campaign against Iraq might well make necessary. And besides, laying the appropriate military, political, diplomatic, and economic groundwork for an invasion will take considerable time and effort.

Nevertheless, those calling for an immediate attack on Iraq make a legitimate point. Too much delay could be as problematic as too little, because it would risk the momentum gained from the victory over Afghanistan. Today the shock of the September 11 attacks is still fresh and the U.S. government and public are ready to make sacrifices—while the rest of the world recognizes American anger and may be leery of getting on the wrong side of it. The longer the wait before an invasion, the harder it will be to muster domestic and international support for it, even though the reason for invading would have little or nothing to do with Iraq's connection to terrorism. And over time the effort to take down al Qaeda could actually exacerbate the problems with containment, since some of America's partners in that effort want to loosen rather than tighten the noose on the Iraqi regime and may try to use the leverage of their cooperation with us to stall any bold moves. The United States can afford to wait a little while before turning to Saddam, in other words, but not indefinitely.

Even when a policy cannot be sustained forever, it often makes sense to spin out its final stages for as long as possible. This is not the case with the containment of Iraq today. The last two years have witnessed a dramatic erosion of the constraints on the Iraqi regime. The Bush administration's initial solution to this problem, the smart sanctions plan, would be little more than a Band-Aid and even so could not find general acceptance. If no more serious action is taken, the United States and the world at large may soon confront a nuclear-armed Saddam. At that point the danger would be obvious to all, but it would be infinitely more difficult to confront. Taking down al Qaeda should indeed be the priority of the moment, and using half-measures, such as the Afghan approach, against Saddam would be a mistake. But these should not become permanent excuses for inaction. We may tarry, but Saddam will not.

This article is part of the Foreign Affairs Iraq Retrospective.

Iraq: The Logic of Disengagement

Edward N. Luttwak

WITHDRAW NOW

Given all that has happened in Iraq to date, the best strategy for the United States is disengagement. This would call for the careful planning and scheduling of the withdrawal of U.S. forces from much of the country—while making due provisions for sharp punitive strikes against any attempt to harass the withdrawing forces. But it would primarily require an intense diplomatic effort, to prepare and conduct parallel negotiations with several parties inside Iraq and out. All have much to lose or gain depending on exactly how the U.S. withdrawal is carried out, and this would give Washington a great deal of leverage that could be used to advance U.S. interests.

The United States cannot threaten to unleash anarchy in Iraq in order to obtain concessions from others, nor can it make transparently conflicting promises about the country's future to different parties. But once it has declared its firm commitment to withdraw—or perhaps, given the widespread conviction that the United States entered Iraq to exploit its resources, once visible physical preparations for an evacuation have begun—the calculus of other parties will change. In a reversal of the usual sequence, the U.S. hand will be strengthened by withdrawal, and Washington may well be able to lay the groundwork for a reasonably stable Iraq. Nevertheless, if key Iraqi factions or Iraq's neighbors are too shortsighted or

Edward N. Luttwak is a Senior Fellow at the Center for Strategic and International Studies.

blinded by resentment to cooperate in their own best interests, the withdrawal should still proceed, with the United States making such favorable or unfavorable arrangements for each party as will most enhance the future credibility of U.S. diplomacy.

The United States has now abridged its vastly ambitious project of creating a veritable Iraqi democracy to pursue the much more realistic aim of conducting some sort of general election. In the meantime, however, it has persisted in futile combat against factions that should be confronting one another instead. A strategy of disengagement would require bold, risk-taking statecraft of a high order, and much diplomatic competence in its execution. But it would be soundly based on the most fundamental of realities: geography that alone ensures all other parties are far more exposed to the dangers of an anarchical Iraq than is the United States itself.

SPAIN, NAPLES, AND IRAQ

If Iraq could indeed be transformed into a successful democracy by a more prolonged occupation, as Germany and Japan were after 1945, then of course any disengagement would be a great mistake. In both of those countries, however, by the time U.S. occupation forces arrived the local populations were already thoroughly disenthralled from violent ideologies, and so they eagerly collaborated with their occupiers to construct democratic institutions. Unfortunately, because of the hostile sentiments of the Iraqi population, the relevant precedents for Iraq are far different.

The very word "guerrilla" acquired its present meaning from the ferocious insurgency of the illiterate Spanish poor against their would-be liberators under the leadership of their traditional oppressors. On July 6, 1808, King Joseph of Spain presented a draft constitution that for the first time in Spain's history offered an independent judiciary, freedom of the press, and the abolition of the remaining feudal privileges of the aristocracy and the church. Ecclesiastical overlords still owned 3,148 towns and villages, which were inhabited by some of Europe's most wretched tenants. Yet the Spanish peasantry did not rise to demand the immediate implementation of the new constitution. Instead, they obeyed the priests, who summoned them to fight against the ungodly innovations of the foreign invader—for Joseph was the brother of Napoleon Bonaparte and had been placed on the Spanish throne by French troops a month earlier. That was all that mattered for most Spaniards—not what was proposed, but who proposed it.

By then the French should have known better. In 1799 the same thing had happened in Naples, whose liberals, supported by the French, were massacred by the very peasants and plebeians they wanted to emancipate, mustered into a militia of the "Holy Faith" by Cardinal Fabrizio Ruffo (the scion, coincidentally, of Calabria's most powerful landowning family). Ruffo easily persuaded his followers that all promises of merely material betterment were irrelevant, because the real aim of the French and the liberals was to destroy the Catholic religion in the service of Satan. Spain's clergy repeated Ruffo's ploy, and their illiterate followers could not know that the very first clause of Joseph's draft constitution had declared the Roman Apostolic Catholic church the only one allowed in Spain.

The same dynamic is playing itself out in Iraq now, down to the ineffectual enshrinement of Islam in the draft constitution and the emergence of truculent clerical warlords. Since the U.S. invasion in 2003, both Shiite and Sunni clerics have been repeating over and over again that the Americans and their mostly "Christian" allies are in Iraq to destroy Islam in its cultural heartland, as well as to steal the country's oil. The clerics dismiss all talk of democracy and human rights by the invaders as mere hypocrisy—except for women's rights, which are promoted in earnest, the clerics say, to induce Iraqi daughters and wives to dishonor their families by aping the shameless disobedience of Western women.

The vast majority of Iraqis, assiduous mosque-goers and semi-literate at best, naturally believe their religious leaders. The alternative would be to believe what for them is entirely incomprehensible: that foreigners have been unselfishly expending their own blood and treasure to help them. As opinion polls and countless incidents demonstrate, Americans and their allies are widely hated as the worst of invaders, out to rob Muslim Iraqis not only of their territory and oil, but also of their religion and family honor.

The most direct and visible effects of these sentiments are the deadly attacks against the occupiers and their Iraqi auxiliaries, the aiding and abetting of such attacks, and their gleeful celebration by impromptu crowds of spectators. When the victims are members of the Iraqi police or National Guard, as is often the case these days, bystanders, family members, and local clerics routinely accuse the Americans of being the attackers—usually by missile strikes that cleverly simulate car bombs. As to why the Americans would want to kill Iraqis whom they are themselves recruiting, training, and paying, no explanation is offered, because no obligation is felt to unravel each and every subplot of the dark Christian conspiracy against Iraq, the Arab world, and Islam.

It is the indirect effects of the insurgency, though, that have ended whatever hopes of genuine democratization may still linger. The mass instruction of Germans and Japanese about the norms and modes of democratic governance, already much facilitated by pre-existing if imperfect democratic institutions, was advanced by mass media of all kinds as well as by countless educational efforts. The work was done by local teachers, preachers, journalists, and publicists who adopted as their own the democratic values proclaimed by the occupiers. But the locals were recruited, instructed, motivated, and guided by occupation political officers, whose own cultural understanding was enhanced by much communing with ordinary Germans and Japanese. In Iraq, by contrast, none of this has occurred. An already difficult task has been made altogether impossible by the refusal of Iraqi teachers, journalists, and publicists—let alone preachers—to be instructed and to instruct others in democratic ways. In any case, unlike Germany or Japan after 1945, Iraq after 2003 never became secure enough for occupation personnel to operate effectively, let alone to carry out mass political education in every city and town, as was done in Germany and Japan.

NO DEMOCRATS, NO DEMOCRACY

Of course, many Iraqis would deny the need for any such instruction, viewing democracy as a simple affair that any child can understand. That is certainly the opinion of the spokesmen of Grand Ayatollah Ali Sistani, for example. They have insistently advocated early elections in Iraq, brushing aside the need for procedural and substantive preparations as basic as the compilation of voter rolls, and seeing no need to allow time for the gathering of consensus by structured political parties. However moderate he may be, the pronouncements attributed to Sistani reveal a confusion between democracy and the dictatorial rule of the majority, for they imply that whoever wins 50.01 percent of the vote should have all of the governing power. That much became clear when Sistani's spokesmen vehemently rejected Kurdish demands for constitutional guarantees of minority rights. Shiite majority rule could thus end up being as undemocratic as the traditional Sunni-Arab ascendancy was.

The plain fact is that there are not enough aspiring democrats in Iraq to sustain democratic institutions. The Shiite majority includes cosmopolitan figures, but by far its greater part has expressed in every possible way a strong preference for clerical leadership. The clerics, in turn, reject any elected assembly that would be free to legislate without their supervision—and could thus legalize, for example, the drinking of alcohol or the freedom to change one's religion. The Sunni-Arab minority, for its part, has dominated Iraq from the time it was formed into a state, and its leaders have consistently rejected democracy in principle because they refuse to accept a subordinate status. As for the Kurds, they have administered their separate de facto autonomies with considerable success, but it is significant that they have not even attempted to hold elections for themselves, preferring clan and tribal loyalties to the individualism of representative democracy.

Accordingly, although elections of some kind can still be held on schedule, they are unlikely to be followed by the emergence of a functioning representative assembly, let alone an effective cohesive government of democratic temper. It follows that the United States has been depleting its military strength, diplomatic leverage, and treasure to pursue a worthy but unrealistic aim.

Yet Iraq cannot simply be evacuated, its fledgling government abandoned to face emboldened Baath loyalists and Sunni-Arab revanchists with their many armed groups, local and foreign Islamists with their terrorist skills, and whatever Shiite militias are left out of the government. In such a contest, the government, with its newly raised security forces of doubtful loyalty, is unlikely to prevail. Nor are the victors likely to divide the country peacefully among themselves; civil war of one kind or another would almost certainly follow. An anarchical Iraq would both threaten the stability of neighboring countries and offer opportunities for their interference—which might even escalate to the point of outright invasions by Iran, or Turkey, or both, initiating new cycles of resistance, repression, and violence.

HOW TO AVOID A ROUT

The probable consequences of abandoning Iraq are so bleak, in fact, that few are willing to contemplate them. That is a mistake. It is precisely because unpredictable mayhem is so predictable that the United States might be able to disengage from Iraq at little cost, or perhaps even advantageously.

To see how disengagement from Iraq might be achieved with few adverse effects or even turned into something of a success, it is useful to approach its undoubted complications by first considering the much simpler case of a plain military retreat. A retreat is notoriously the most difficult of military operations to pull off successfully. At worst, it can degenerate into a disastrous rout. But a well-calculated retreat not only can extricate a force from a difficult situation, but in doing so can actually turn the tide of battle by luring the enemy beyond the limits of its strength until it is overstretched, unbalanced, and ripe for defeat. In Iraq, the United States faces no single enemy army it can exhaust in this way, but rather a number of different enemies whose mutual hostility now lies dormant but could be catalyzed by a well-crafted disengagement.

Because Iraq is under foreign occupation, Islamic, nationalist, and pan-Arab sentiments currently prevail over denominational identities, inducing Sunni and Shiite Arabs to unite against the invaders. So long as Iraqis of all kinds believe that the United States has no intention of withdrawing, they can attack American forces to express their nationalism or Islamism without calculating the consequences for themselves of a post- American Iraq. That is why Moktada al-Sadr's Shiite militia felt free to attack the U.S. troops that elsewhere were fighting Sunnis bent on restoring their ancestral supremacy, and why its actions were applauded by the clerics and the Shiite population at large. Yet if faced with the prospect of an imminent U.S. withdrawal, Shiite clerics and their followers would have to confront the equally imminent threat of the Baath loyalist and Sunni fighters—the only Iraqis with recent combat experience, and the least likely to accept Shiite clerical rule.

That is why by moving to withdraw the United States could secure what the occupation has never had: the active support of its greatest beneficiaries, the Shiites. What Washington needs from them is a total cessation of violence against the coalition throughout Iraq, full cooperation with the interim government in the conduct of elections, and the suspension of all forms of support for other resisters. Given that there is already some acquiescence and even cooperation, this would not require a full reversal in Shiite attitudes.

WITH FRIENDS LIKE THESE

Iran, for its part, has much to fear from anarchy in Iraq, which would present it with more dangers than opportunities. At present, because the Iranians think the United States is determined to remain in Iraq no matter what, the hard-liners in Iran's government feel free to pursue their anti-American vendetta by political subversion, by arming and training al-Sadr's militia, and by encouraging the Syrians to favor the infiltration of Islamist terrorists into Iraq.

Anarchy in Iraq would threaten not merely Iran's stability, but also its territorial integrity. Minorities account for more than half the population, yet the government of Iran is not pluralist at all. It functions as an exclusively Persian empire that suppresses all other ethnic identities and imposes the exclusive use of Farsi in public education, thus condemning all others to illiteracy in their mother tongues. Moreover, not only the Baha'i but also more combative heterodox Muslims are now persecuted. Except for some Kurds and Azeris, no minority is actively rebellious as yet, but chaos in Iraq could energize communal loyalties in Iran (especially among the Kurds and the Arabs). An anarchical Iraq would offer bases for Iranian dissidents and exiles, at a time when the theocratic regime is certainly weaker than it once was: its political support has measurably waned, its revolutionary and religious authority is now a distant memory, and its continued hold on power depends increasingly on naked force—and the regime knows it.

Once the United States commits to a disengagement from Iraq, therefore, a suitably discreet dialogue with Iranian rulers should be quite productive. Washington would not need to demand much from the Iranians: only the end of subversion, arms trafficking, hostile propaganda, and Hezbollah infiltration in Iraq. Ever since the 1979 revolution, the United States has often wished for restraint from the theocratic rulers of Iran but has generally lacked the means to obtain it. Even the simultaneous presence of U.S. combat forces on both the eastern and western frontiers of Iran has had little impact on the actual conduct of the regime, which usually diverges from its more moderate declared policies. But what the entry of troops could not achieve, a withdrawal might, for it would expose the inherent vulnerability to dissidents of an increasingly isolated regime.

As an ally of long standing, Turkey is in a wholly different category. After hindering the initial invasion of Iraq, it has helped the occupation in important ways—but it has still done less than it might have done. The reason is that Turkish policy has focused to an inordinate extent on the enhancement of Iraq's Turkmen minority, driven not by a dubious ethnic solidarity (they are Azeris, not Turks) but by a desire to weaken the Iraqi Kurds. The Iraqi

Turkmen are concentrated in and around the city of Kirkuk, possession of which secures control of a good part of Iraq's oil-production capacity. By providing military aid to the Turkmen, the Turkish government is therefore assisting the anti- Kurdish coalition in Kirkuk, which includes Sunnis actively fighting Americans. This amounts to indirect action against the United States. There is no valid justification for such activities, which have increased communal violence and facilitated the sabotage of oil installations.

Like others, the Turkish government must have calculated that with the United States committed to the occupation, the added burden placed on Iraq's stability by their support of the Turkmen would make no difference. With disengagement, however, a negotiation could and should begin to see what favors might be exchanged between Ankara and Washington—in order to ensure that the U.S. withdrawal benefits Turkish interests while Turks stop making trouble in Iraqi Kurdistan.

Even Kuwait, whose very existence depends on American military power, now does very little to help the occupation and the interim Iraqi government. The Kuwaiti Red Crescent Society has sent the odd truckload of food into Iraq, and a gift of some $60 million has been announced, though not necessarily delivered. Given Kuwait's exceptionally high oil revenues, however, not to mention the large revenues of Kuwaiti subcontractors working under Pentagon logistics contracts, this is less than paltry. The serious amounts of aid that Kuwait could well afford would allow the interim government to extend its authority and help the postelection government to resolve differences and withstand the attacks destined to come against it. In procuring such aid, it would not take much reminding that if the United States cannot effect a satisfactory disengagement, the Kuwaitis will be more than 10,000 miles closer to the ensuing anarchy than the Americans themselves.

As for the Saudi regime, its relentlessly ambiguous attitude is exemplified by its July 2003 offer of a contingent of "Islamic" troops to help garrison Iraq. Made with much fanfare, the offer sounded both generous and courageous. Then it turned out that the troops in question were not to be Saudi at all—in other words, the Saudis were promising to send the troops of other, unspecified Muslim countries—and these imaginary troops were to be sent on condition that an equal number of U.S. troops be withdrawn.

In the realm of action rather than empty words, the Saudis have not actually tried to worsen U.S. difficulties in Iraq, but they have not been especially helpful, either. As with Kuwait, their exploding oil revenues could underwrite substantial gifts to the Iraqi government, both before and after the elections. But Riyadh could do even more. All evidence indicates that Saudi volunteers have been infiltrating into Iraq in greater numbers than any other nationality. They join the other Islamists whose attacks kill many Iraqis and some Americans. Saudi Arabia and Iraq share a border along which there are few and rather languid patrols, rare control posts, and no aerial surveillance, even though it could be readily provided. And the Saudis could try harder to limit the flow of money from Saudi jihad enthusiasts and do more to discourage the religious decrees that sanction the killing of Americans in Iraq.

As it is, the Saudi authorities are doing none of this. Yet an anarchical Iraq would endanger the Saudi regime's already fragile security, not least by providing their opponents all the bases they need and offering Iran a tempting playground for expansion. Here too, therefore, hard-headed negotiations about the modalities of a U.S. withdrawal would seem to hold out possibilities for significant improvements.

The Syrian regime, finally, could also be engaged in a dialogue, one in which the United States presents two scenarios. The first is a well-prepared disengagement conducted with much support from inside and outside Iraq that leaves it with a functioning government. The second is the same thing accompanied by punitive action against Syria if it attempts to sabotage that outcome—much easier to do once U.S. forces are no longer tied down in Iraq. For all its anti-American bluster, the Syrian regime is unlikely to risk confrontation, especially when so little is asked of it: a closure of the Syria-Iraq border to extremists and the end of Hezbollah activities in Iraq (funded by Iran but authorized by Syria).

Of all Iraq's neighbors, only Jordan has been straightforwardly cooperative, incidentally without compromising any of its own sovereign interests.

THE ULTIMATE LOGIC OF DISENGAGEMENT

Even if the negotiations here advocated fail to yield all they might—indeed, even if they do not yield much at all—the disengagement should still occur, and not only to live up to the initial commitment to withdraw. Given the bitter Muslim hostility to the presence of U.S. troops—labeled "Christian Crusaders" by the preachers—their continued deployment in large numbers can only undermine the legitimacy of any U.S.-supported Iraqi government. With Iraq more like Spain in 1808 than like Germany or Japan after 1945, any democracy it sustains is bound to be more veneer than substance. Its chances of survival will be much higher if pan-Arab nationalists, Islamists, and foreign meddlers are neutralized by diplomacy and disengagement. Leaving behind a major garrison would only evoke continuing hostility to both Americans and Iraqi democrats. Once U.S. soldiers have left Iraqi cities, towns, and villages, some could remain a while in remote desert bases to fight off full-scale military attacks against the government—but even this could incite opposition, as happened in Saudi Arabia.

A strategy of disengagement would require much skill in conducting parallel negotiations. But its risks are actually lower than the alternative of an indefinite occupation, and its benefits might surprise us. An anarchical Iraq is a far greater danger to those in or near it than to the United States. It is time to collect on the difference.

This article is part of the Foreign Affairs Iraq Retrospective.

How to Win in Iraq

Andrew F. Krepinevich Jr.

A FALTERING EFFORT

Despite the Bush administration's repeated declarations of its commitment to success in Iraq, the results of current policy there are not encouraging. After two years, Washington has made little progress in defeating the insurgency or providing security for Iraqis, even as it has overextended the U.S. Army and eroded support for the war among the American public. Although withdrawing now would be a mistake, simply "staying the course," by all current indications, will not improve matters either. Winning in Iraq will require a new approach.

The basic problem is that the United States and its coalition partners have never settled on a strategy for defeating the insurgency and achieving their broader objectives. On the political front, they have been working to create a democratic Iraq, but that is a goal, not a strategy. On the military front, they have sought to train Iraqi security forces and turn the war over to them. As President George W. Bush has stated, "Our strategy can be summed up this way: as the Iraqis stand up, we will stand down." But the president is describing a withdrawal plan rather than a strategy.

Without a clear strategy in Iraq, moreover, there is no good way to gauge progress. Senior political and military leaders have thus repeatedly made overly optimistic or even contradictory declarations. In May of 2004, for example, following the insurgent takeover of Fallujah, General Richard Myers, chair of the Joint Chiefs

ANDREW F. KREPINEVICH, JR., is Executive Director of the Center for Strategic and Budgetary Assessments and Distinguished Visiting Professor of Public Policy at George Mason University. He is the author of The Army and Vietnam.

of Staff, stated, "I think we're on the brink of success here." Six months later, before last November's offensive to recapture the city, General John Abizaid, the commander of U.S. forces in Iraq and Afghanistan, said, "When we win this fight—and we will win—there will be nowhere left for the insurgents to hide." Following the recapture, Lieutenant General John Sattler, the Marine commander in Iraq, declared that the coalition had "broken the back of the insurgency." Yet in the subsequent months, the violence continued unabated. Nevertheless, seven months later Vice President Dick Cheney claimed that the insurgency was in its "last throes," even as Lieutenant General John Vines, commander of the multinational corps in Iraq, was conceding, "We don't see the insurgency expanding or contracting right now." Most Americans agree with this less optimistic assessment: according to the most recent polls, nearly two-thirds think the coalition is "bogged down."

The administration's critics, meanwhile, have offered as their alternative "strategy" an accelerated timetable for withdrawal. They see Iraq as another Vietnam and advocate a similar solution: pulling out U.S. troops and hoping for the best. The costs of such premature disengagement would likely be calamitous. The insurgency could morph into a bloody civil war, with the significant involvement of both Syria and Iran. Radical Islamists would see the U.S. departure as a victory, and the ensuing chaos would drive up oil prices.

Instead of a timetable for withdrawal, the United States needs a real strategy built around the principles of counterinsurgency warfare. To date, U.S. forces in Iraq have largely concentrated their efforts on hunting down and killing insurgents. The idea of such operations is to erode the enemy's strength by killing fighters more quickly than replacements can be recruited. Although it is too early to tell for sure whether this approach will ultimately bring success, its current record is not good: even when an attack manages to inflict serious insurgent casualties, there is little or no enduring improvement in security once U.S. forces withdraw from the area.

Instead, U.S. and Iraqi forces should adopt an "oil-spot strategy" in Iraq, which is essentially the opposite approach. Rather than focusing on killing insurgents, they should concentrate on providing security and opportunity to the Iraqi people, thereby denying insurgents the popular support they need. Since the U.S. and Iraqi armies cannot guarantee security to all of Iraq simultaneously, they should start by focusing on certain key areas and then, over time, broadening the effort—hence the image of an expanding oil spot. Such a strategy would have a good chance of success. But it would require a protracted commitment of U.S. resources, a willingness to risk more casualties in the short term, and an enduring U.S. presence in Iraq, albeit at far lower force levels than are engaged at present. If U.S. policymakers and the American public are unwilling to make such a commitment, they should be prepared to scale down their goals in Iraq significantly.

THE FACE OF THE INSURGENCY

The insurgency plaguing Iraq has three sources. One is the inexplicable lack of U.S. postwar planning. The security vacuum that followed the collapse of Saddam Hussein's regime gave hostile elements the opportunity to organize, and the poorly designed and slowly implemented reconstruction plan provided the insurgents with a large pool of unemployed Iraqis from which to recruit. The second source is Iraq's tradition of rule by those best able to seize power through violent struggle. Washington's muddled signals have created the impression that American troops may soon depart, opening the way to an Iraqi power struggle. (This is why the Shiite Arabs and the Kurds, even though they generally support the new government, have refused to disband their own militias.) The third source of the insurgency is the fact that jihadists have made Iraq a major theater in their war against the United States, abetted by the absence of security in Iraq and the presence of some 140,000 U.S. "targets."

The insurgency is dominated by two groups: Sunni Arab Baathists and foreign jihadists. Although it is difficult to measure their strength precisely, the former group is clearly larger, numbering perhaps 20,000, while the jihadists are estimated to number in the low hundreds. The Baathists—former members of Saddam's ruling elite—hope to restore themselves to power. The jihadists want to inflict a defeat on the United States, deal a blow to its influence in the region, and establish a radical Islamist state in Iraq.

Both insurgent camps know they cannot defeat the U.S.-led coalition militarily. Their best chance of success is to wait for a premature U.S. withdrawal and then spark a coup, in which a small, well-disciplined group with foreign backing seizes power from a weak, demoralized regime. Toward this end, the insurgents are fighting to perpetuate disorder and to prevent the establishment of a legitimate, democratic Iraqi government. By creating an atmosphere of intimidation, insecurity, and despair, they hope to undermine support for the government. Brazen attacks on its leaders and police send a chilling message to the Iraqi people: If the government cannot even protect its own, how can it protect you? Sabotage of Iraq's national infrastructure underscores the government's failure to provide basic services such as water and electricity and to sustain the oil production on which Iraq's welfare depends. By inflicting casualties on U.S. forces at the same time, the insurgents seek to raise the cost of continued U.S. involvement and weaken support for the war back home—thereby hastening a U.S. withdrawal.

The insurgents have proved themselves to be resilient and resourceful, but they have also shown serious weaknesses. Compared with the United States' opponents in Vietnam, they are a relatively small and isolated group; the Iraqi rebels number no more than a few tens of thousands, whereas the ranks of the Vietnamese Communists were composed of roughly ten times that number. Iraqi insurgents rarely fight in groups as large as 100; in Vietnam, U.S. forces often encountered well-coordinated enemy formations of far greater size. The Vietnamese Communists, veterans of over two decades of nearly continuous war against the Japanese, the French, and the South Vietnamese, were also far better trained and led than the Iraqi insurgents and enjoyed external backing from China and the Soviet Union. The support provided to the insurgents by Iran, Syria, and radical Islamists elsewhere pales in comparison.

The Iraqi insurgents are also relatively isolated from the Iraqi people. Sunni Arab Muslims comprise the overwhelming majority of insurgent forces but account for only 20 percent of Iraq's population, and the jihadists are mostly foreigners. Neither insurgent movement has any chance of stimulating a broad-based uprising that involves Arab Shiites and Kurds. Indeed, despite the hardships endured by the Iraqi people, there has been nothing even approaching a mass revolt against the U.S.-led forces or the interim Iraqi government. This is not surprising, for the insurgents have no positive message with which to inspire popular support. A Baathist restoration would mean a return to the misery of Saddam's rule, and the jihadists would do to Iraq what radical Islamists have done in Afghanistan and Iran: introduce a reign of terror and repression.

The insurgency's success, accordingly, depends on continued disorder to forestall the creation of a stable, democratic Iraq and erode the coalition's willingness to persist and prevail. The insurgents believe the coalition lacks staying power, citing as evidence the U.S. withdrawals from Lebanon following the 1983 bombing of the Marine barracks in Beirut and from Somalia a decade later after 18 U.S. servicemen were killed. The Baathist insurgents hope that if they succeed in outlasting the Americans, support from Syria and other Arab states will enable them to topple the new regime. This would likely trigger a civil war, with Shiite Arab Iraqis supported by Iran. Radical Islamists would have perhaps their best chance of seizing power under such chaotic conditions.

CENTERS OF GRAVITY

In conventional warfare, the enemy's military forces and capital city are often considered its centers of gravity, meaning that losing either would spell defeat. In the Iraq war, for example, the coalition concentrated on destroying Saddam's Republican Guard and capturing Baghdad. But the centers of gravity in counterinsurgency warfare are completely different, and focusing efforts on defeating the enemy's military forces through traditional forms of combat is a mistake.

The current fight has three centers of gravity: the Iraqi people, the American people, and the American soldier. The insurgents have recognized this, making them their primary targets. For the United States, the key to securing each one is winning "hearts and minds." The Iraqi people must believe that their government offers them a better life than the insurgents do, and they must think that the government will prevail. If they have doubts on either score, they will withhold their support. The American people must believe that the war is worth the sacrifice, in lives and treasure, and think that progress is being made. If the insurgents manage to erode their will, Washington will be forced to abandon the infant regime in Baghdad before it is capable of standing on its own. Finally, the American soldier must believe that the war is worth the sacrifice and think that there is progress toward victory. Unlike in Vietnam, the United States is waging war with an all-volunteer military, which gives the American soldier (or marine) a "vote" in the conflict. With over 150,000 troops in Iraq and Afghanistan, soldiers must rotate back into those war zones at a high rate. If confidence in the war wanes, veterans will vote with their feet by refusing to reenlist and prospective new recruits will avoid signing up in the first place. If this occurs, the United States will be unable to sustain anything approaching its current effort in Iraq. A precipitous reduction in U.S. forces could further undermine the resolve of both the American and the Iraqi people. At present, U.S. Army and Marine Corps reenlistment rates are strong. Army recruiting, however, is down substantially.

The insurgents have a clear advantage when it comes to this fight: they only need to win one of the centers of gravity to succeed, whereas the United States must secure all three. Making matters even more complicated for the coalition, a Catch-22 governs the fight against the insurgency: efforts designed to secure one center of gravity may undermine the prospects of securing the others. For example, increased U.S. troop deployments to Iraq—which require that greater resources be spent and troops be rotated in and out more frequently—might increase security for the Iraqi people but erode support for the war among the U.S. public and the military. This risk is especially great given the nature of the current U.S. operations against the insurgents. They put too great an emphasis on destroying insurgent forces and minimizing U.S. casualties and too little on providing enduring security to the Iraqi people; too much effort into sweeping maneuvers with no enduring presence and too little into the effective coordination of security and reconstruction efforts; and too high a priority on quickly fielding large numbers of Iraqi security forces and too low a priority on ensuring their effectiveness.

The key to securing the centers of gravity in the current war is to recognize that U.S. forces have overwhelming advantages in terms of combat power and mobility but a key disadvantage in terms of intelligence. If they know who the insurgents are and where they are, they can quickly suppress the insurgency. The Iraqi people are the best source of this intelligence. But U.S. forces and their allies can only gain this knowledge by winning locals' hearts and minds—that is, by convincing them that the insurgents' defeat is in their interest and that they can share intelligence about them without fear of insurgent reprisals.

HISTORY LESSONS

Insurgencies are nearly as old as warfare itself, so there is no shortage of past counterinsurgency strategies to draw on. The Romans suppressed rebellions with such ferocity and ruthlessness that it was said they would "create a desert and call it peace."

The British often maintained order through a divide-and-conquer strategy. They would support one of several factions vying for power, and in return for this support the favored group would respect British interests in that part of the world. Neither of these strategies is attractive today. The Roman approach clearly conflicts with American values, and the British strategy would lead to a client-sponsor relationship with a nondemocratic regime—hardly what the Bush administration hopes to foster in Iraq.

During the Vietnam War, U.S. strategy focused on killing insurgents at the expense of winning hearts and minds. This search-and-destroy strategy ultimately failed, but it evidently continues to exert a strong pull on the U.S. military, as indicated by statements like that of a senior army commander in Iraq who declared, "[I] don't think we will put much energy into trying the old saying, 'win the hearts and minds.' I don't look at it as one of the metrics of success." Having left the business of waging counterinsurgency warfare over 30 years ago, the U.S. military is running the risk of failing to do what is needed most (win Iraqis' hearts and minds) in favor of what it has traditionally done best (seek out the enemy and destroy him). Thus, U.S. forces have recently pushed forward with more offensive operations of this type in western Iraq, which has produced some insurgent casualties but had a negligible effect on overall security.

The oil-spot strategy, in contrast, focuses on establishing security for the population precisely for the sake of winning hearts and minds. In the 1950s, the British used it successfully in Malaya, as did the Filipinos against the Huk insurgents. Given the centers of gravity and the limits of U.S. forces in Iraq, an oil-spot approach—in which operations would be oriented around securing the population and then gradually but inexorably expanded to increase control over contested areas—could work.

Coalition forces and local militias, such as the Kurdish Pesh Merga, now provide a high level of security in 14 of Iraq's 18 provinces. These areas comprise the country's true "Green Zone" (the term normally used to describe the heavily fortified part of Baghdad where U.S. headquarters are located). In these provinces, people lead relatively normal and secure lives. The rest of the country—the "Red Zone"—is made up of the generally unsecured provinces of Anbar, Baghdad, Nineveh, and Salah ad Din, each of which has a sizable or dominant Sunni Arab population. The oil-spot campaign should start by enhancing security in the Green Zone. The U.S. and Iraqi governments should also focus reconstruction efforts here, in order to reward loyalty to the government and to minimize "security premium" expenses on projects.

To start, U.S. and coalition forces must do much more to aid and develop the capabilities of their Iraqi counterparts in counterinsurgency operations: training them, embedding U.S. soldiers and marines in Iraqi units, and providing U.S. quick-reaction forces to support the Iraqis, if needed. The embedding effort should be far more extensive than currently planned, and some of the U.S. Army's best soldiers should be assigned to this initiative. It would involve some risk, since embedded U.S. personnel are likely to suffer more casualties than they would in all-U.S. units. But the payoff would be high as well.

The challenges associated with training Iraqi security forces are well documented, but the United States could still dramatically improve on its current efforts. Embedding more and higher-quality U.S. soldiers in Iraqi units would be like inserting a steel reinforcing rod into hardening concrete. A higher number of embedded soldiers would support the training of Iraqi officers, as well as facilitate the identification and advancement of capable Iraqi leaders (and weed out substandard ones). Finally, by concentrating Iraqi forces in generally secure areas and in a few areas selected for security "offensives," the oil-spot strategy would minimize the risk that newly trained Iraqi units will find themselves in over their heads and without adequate support.

The U.S. high command must also end the pernicious practice of rotating senior military and civilian leaders in and out of Iraq as though they are interchangeable. Generals who have demonstrated competence in dealing with insurgents in Afghanistan and Iraq have been recalled to stateside duty. Such officers should be promoted and retained in Iraq for an extended period. Those who fail should be rotated back home and replaced. As history has shown time and again, capable leaders are "force multipliers": they greatly enhance the effectiveness of the troops under their command.

The offensives in the oil-spot strategy should consist of efforts to expand the Green Zone by securing, over time, more and more of the Red Zone. In each phase, both security and reconstruction resources would go to areas selected for these offensives. Since forces and resources are limited—and because laying the foundation for enduring security in each currently unsecured area would take considerable time, likely half a year or longer—oil-spot offensives would typically be protracted in nature.

Each offensive would begin with Iraqi army units and their embedded U.S. advisers sweeping through the target area and clearing it of any major insurgent forces. These units would then break up into smaller formations and take up positions in towns (or, in the case of cities, sectors) of the cleared area, providing local security. National police would then arrive and begin security patrols and the vetting and training of local police and paramilitary security forces. As these efforts developed, Iraqi army units would switch to intensive patrolling along the oil spot's periphery to deflect insurgent threats to the newly secured area. A quick-reaction force made up of U.S. or Iraqi army units would deal with any insurgent penetration of the patrol zone. Iraqi and U.S. intelligence operatives would begin the process of infiltrating local insurgent cells and recruiting local Iraqis to do the same. Although current efforts at infiltration have produced spotty results, the oil-spot strategy would give U.S. and Iraqi intelligence forces the time needed to succeed by committing coalition forces to provide an enduring level of security.

These security operations would facilitate reconstruction, offering Iraqis the promise of a better life. Sustained security would also ensure that the benefits of reconstruction would endure, rather than be sabotaged by the insurgents. It would facilitate social reform—for example, enabling women to attend school without fear of retribution from radical Islamists. It would also provide time for the proper vetting and training of local security forces before they assumed their responsibilities. Finally, enduring security would help to convince the local population that the government is serious about protecting them. The overall objective, of course, would be winning their active support, whereupon they would presumably begin providing the government with intelligence on those insurgents who have "gone to ground" in the secured area. Once the population sees the benefits of security and reconstruction—and not until then—local elections could be held.

Given limited military and financial resources, the targets for oil-spot offensives would have to be carefully chosen. Two attractive targets would be Baghdad and the northern city of Mosul. Both are key political and economic centers that border relatively secure areas. As Iraq's capital, Baghdad has great symbolic value. And both areas are within the operational area of U.S. forces, the most capable in the coalition.

U.S. and Iraqi forces should refine their choices by targeting those areas where they can find tribal allies—and should design reconstruction efforts to ensure that the cooperative local sheik receives "credit" for his help in the eyes of his tribe. Providing such credit would increase the incentives for the tribe to help ensure that reconstruction succeeds, and it might help persuade tribes to provide intelligence on potential acts of sabotage or even to actively support security operations.

Once local forces are ready to assume principal responsibility for local security, most of the Iraqi army units in the area, the national police, and their U.S. supporters should expand the oil spot further. Some quick-reaction forces, however, should remain in the initial oil-spot area to guarantee that the local security forces have prompt support if needed.

Although securing Green Zone targets as well key national infrastructure and previously secured areas should be the military's first priority, the four unsecured provinces cannot simply be abandoned to the insurgents. Small, extended patrols of U.S. (and, with time, Iraqi) Special Operations forces in the Red Zone should be undertaken to provide intelligence and early warning of significant insurgent activities, while denying insurgents sanctuary and limiting their ability to rest, refit, and plan. If the insurgents attempt to occupy a major town or city, as they did in Fallujah, U.S. and Iraqi forces should mount a punitive expedition to drive them out. Such operations, however, must always remain subordinate to the overall oil-spot strategy, focused on protecting the population, not pursuing insurgent forces.

An important advantage to the oil-spot strategy, given growing concerns over U.S. Army recruiting problems and declining U.S. public support, is that it should be possible to execute the strategy, including the Baghdad and Mosul offensives, with fewer than the 140,000 U.S. troops now in Iraq—120,000 might be sufficient. This 20,000 troop reduction would be possible for several reasons. Substantially increasing the number of U.S. advisers in newly formed Iraqi units would enable these units to become more capable more quickly, and curtailing ill-advised sweep operations would enable U.S. forces to be employed more productively. Retaining capable senior U.S. generals in Iraq for extended periods, meanwhile, would dramatically enhance military effectiveness, even at somewhat lower force levels.

THE GRAND BARGAIN

Lieutenant General Sir Gerald Templer, Britain's high commissioner and director of operations during the Malayan insurgency in the 1950s, observed that the political and military sides of counterinsurgency must be "completely and utterly interrelated." So, too, must they be in Iraq. While U.S. military operations take the form of the oil-spot campaign, political efforts should aim to strike a grand bargain with the Iraqi people. This grand bargain would lay the foundation for the gradual development of the broad base needed to sustain an Iraqi democracy.

The grand bargain would cut across key Iraqi religious and ethnic groups and across key tribal and familial units. Its underlying assumptions would be that there are significant elements of each major ethnic and religious group willing to support a democratic, unified Iraq; that a sufficiently broad coalition can be formed, over time, to achieve this end; and that the United States is willing to undertake a long-term effort, lasting a decade or longer, to ensure the grand bargain's success. The Kurds would likely be the easiest to win over. They want the insurgency defeated and a long-term U.S. presence to protect them against Shiite dominance or a Sunni restoration, as well as against external threats from Iran and Turkey. A small, but significant, Sunni element may also want the insurgency defeated, if it can be assured of a long-term U.S. presence to hedge against both Shiite domination (and retribution) and Iranian domination of a Shiite-led government. Like the Kurds, most Shiites want the insurgency defeated. Some are also wary of Iranian attempts to subvert Iraqi independence. These Shiites may also accept a long-term U.S. presence to guard against Iranian subversion and to minimize the risks of a civil war that would threaten their natural advantage in numbers in an Iraqi democracy.

This grand bargain would not seek to win over any one of the principal Iraqi groups entirely, only a substantial portion of each, which combined would provide a critical mass in support of the common objectives mentioned above. Since defeating the insurgency is but one step toward achieving these objectives, each group would have an incentive to have Iraq retain some U.S. forces beyond the insurgency's defeat—something critical to achieving the United States' broader security objectives. Under the grand bargain, in short, Iraqis may find that although having U.S. "occupiers" offends their sense of nationalism, with the existence of a sovereign Iraqi regime they are willing to tolerate a much smaller force as "guests."

Stitching this coalition together would require a good understanding of Iraqi tribal politics. In many areas of Iraq, the tribe and the extended family are the foundation of society, and they represent a sort of alternative to the government. (Saddam deftly manipulated these tribal and familial relationships to sustain his rule.) There are roughly 150 tribes in Iraq of varying size and influence, and at least 75 percent of Iraqis are members of a tribe. Creating a coalition out of these groups would require systematically mapping tribal structures, loyalties, and blood feuds within and among tribal groups; identifying unresolved feuds; detecting the political inclinations of dominant tribes and their sources of power and legitimacy; and determining their ties to tribes in other countries, particularly in Iran, Syria, and Turkey.

To this end, the United States should help the Iraqi government establish an Iraqi Information Service to gather intelligence on the insurgents and penetrate their infrastructure. The service should divide Iraq into regions, sectors, and local grids to focus their efforts, with priority going to those areas that have been secured by or targeted for oil-spot operations. Although U.S. and other coalition forces should monitor and support this effort, the Iraqis themselves, given their superior understanding of local culture, must lead it. Given the unsettled state of Iraqi politics, however, American "Iraqi affairs officers" should also be embedded in Iraqi Information Service units to monitor their activities.

Accurate tribal mapping could guide the formation of alliances between the new Iraqi government and certain tribes and families, improve the vetting of military recruits and civil servants, and enhance intelligence sources on the insurgency's organization and infrastructure. Most important, it would facilitate achieving the grand bargain by identifying the Kurdish, Sunni, and Shiite tribes that would be most likely to support a unified, independent, and democratic Iraqi state. In return, tribal allies should receive more immediate benefits, such as priority in security and reconstruction operations.

There are risks in making allies of tribal groups. Tribal alliances are often ephemeral, and the coalition must be prepared to shift its allegiance back and forth between rival tribes rapidly. There is also the risk of tribes emerging as alternatives to the government. Taking on one tribe as an ally may make enemies out of rival tribes that heretofore were neutral. It will take diligence and expert diplomacy to make this element of the strategy work.

As progress is made in crafting the grand bargain and the first oil-spot offensives are concluded, the strategy would enter its second phase. Phase II would see a significant reduction in U.S. force levels—perhaps to as few as 60,000—reflecting the growing strength of the Iraqi government and security forces and the declining strength of the insurgents. U.S. advisers would begin to be phased out of the most capable Iraqi units. Over time, as the insurgent threat shrank to an insignificant problem, the third phase of the strategy would be implemented: the withdrawal of the U.S. military units and most advisers, save for a residual U.S. military presence numbering perhaps 20,000 troops to deter predators such as Iran and Syria. This U.S. security umbrella would also eliminate Baghdad's need to pursue costly nuclear, chemical, or biological weapons programs. In addition, a residual U.S. presence would discourage any internal Iraqi faction from attempting to overthrow the government.

BETTER METRICS

To date, the Bush administration and its critics alike have often focused on the wrong metrics for measuring progress in the Iraq war. Critics, for example, often use insurgent strength to gauge progress. But it is notoriously difficult to assess accurately insurgent force levels, especially because many Iraqi insurgents are neither full-time participants in the conflict nor true believers in the Baathist or the radical Islamist cause. Rather, they have been forced to support the insurgency or have been co-opted by insurgents, who pay unemployed Iraqis to plant improvised explosive devices (IEDs).

It is also tempting to use the number of combat incidents as a sign of insurgent strength and the lack thereof as a sign of insurgent weakness. This must be done with care. A lack of insurgent activity does not necessarily mean success for the counterinsurgent forces. The number of combat incidents around Fallujah in the summer of 2004 was quite low. Yet this was hardly a measure of the Iraqi government's success. Rather, it was a clear signal of its impotence, since the insurgents were in full control of the city at that time. Conversely, a large number of attacks may reflect the insurgents' weakness. A rash of attacks might result from insurgents' fears that they are losing the war and must do something dramatic to reverse their fortunes. Consider, for example, the spike in violence around the time of the January 2005 elections—violence motivated by the insurgents' fear of the elections, not their growing strength.

Nevertheless, it is worth tracking insurgent activity, not to get a sense of whether progress is being made but to understand the insurgents' priorities and to recognize trends in their behavior. For example, tracking combat incidents could provide insights into trends in the scale of enemy attacks, their level of success, and the insurgents' targeting priorities. These data may also signal a shift in the insurgents' strategy. For example, signs that insurgents were moving away from attacks on government officials could indicate that efforts to protect key government officials were paying off.

To the extent that U.S. casualties erode support for the war among American soldiers and the American public, they are an important metric in gauging progress. But the current casualty rate is well below that suffered in Vietnam, and support among those most in danger—American soldiers and marines—remains strong. Both the U.S. Army and the U.S. Marine Corps are exceeding their reenlistment rates. It is the army's recruitment efforts that are experiencing difficulties, an indication that Americans in general are increasingly reluctant to serve.

More important than casualties when it comes to securing the two American centers of gravity is the "free-rider problem." If Americans think that the Iraqis do not want to fight for their own freedom against undemocratic insurgent movements, U.S. soldiers (and the American people) may become increasingly reluctant to make sacrifices on the behalf of those they perceive to be ungrateful beneficiaries.

There are other, less problematic metrics that could prove useful in measuring the war's progress and taking the pulse of the war's centers of gravity. One is the number of assassinations of government officials and religious leaders. From the population's perspective, if the government cannot even protect its officials, it is difficult to see how it can protect individual citizens. Correspondingly, if the insurgents cannot protect their leaders from being killed or captured, it would likely discourage prospective recruits, who would infer that the rebels could not shield them either. Success here would be a clear indication that the counterinsurgent forces were winning the intelligence battle. Since victory in this sense would very likely mean that individual citizens were stepping forward to provide information, it would also mean that the coalition and the Iraqi government were winning over the "hearts and minds" of the Iraqi people and thus securing a crucial center of gravity.

Another useful metric is the percentage of contacts with the enemy that are initiated by coalition forces. This measurement can gauge progress in the intelligence war, which is a surrogate for popular support in Iraq. A positive trend in this metric would indicate that the population was providing "actionable" intelligence and that the initiative was passing from the insurgent to the counterinsurgent forces. A subset of this metric, the percentage of contacts with the enemy initiated by Iraqi forces, is far superior to counting Iraqi troops in determining the Iraqi security forces' effectiveness. If the percentage of contacts with the enemy that are initiated by Iraqi forces were to increase, and if their share relative to that of other coalition forces were to grow, this would indicate that Iraqi forces are assuming more of the burden for Iraq's security and also winning the people's support. Positive trends in this metric could also encourage greater U.S. popular support, since it would also enable reductions in the number of U.S. troops in Iraq.

Still another useful measure is the percentage of "actionable" intelligence tips received from the population relative to the percentage gained through military surveillance (reconnaissance aircraft or security forces patrols, for example) and government intelligence operatives. An increase in this ratio would indicate that the people share the coalition's objectives and feel secure enough to volunteer information on the insurgents.

Then there are "market metrics." Insurgents have exploited both the unemployed and criminals in seeking support. They often pay Iraqis to plant IEDs and declare bounties for the killing of government officials. Such measures indicate that the insurgency is struggling to expand its ranks and must buy support. It would be helpful to keep track of the "market" in this aspect of the conflict. What are the insurgents offering to those who will plant an IED? What kind of bounty are they placing on the lives of their enemies, and how does that price change over time? The assumption behind these market metrics is that the higher the insurgents' price, the fewer people there are who are willing to support them. Such a reduction in support could indicate success on the part of the coalition and the Iraqi government in improving security, reducing unemployment, and strengthening the popular commitment to the new regime, all of which would leave fewer people vulnerable to persuasion or coercion by the insurgents.

PAYING THE PRICE

No strategy will bring about an end to the insurgency quickly or easily. In that sense, the strategy presented here is the best of a bad lot. It is superior to the current "stay the course" strategy and to following an arbitrary timetable for withdrawing from Iraq, the solution advocated by many of the Bush administration's critics. Its chief virtue is that it reflects an understanding of the war's centers of gravity and attempts to balance the sometimes competing demands of these centers while also securing them.

There will of course be great difficulties in carrying out such a plan. First, creating a coalition for a grand bargain will prove challenging, given the long-standing animosities between segments of the Iraqi population, the Iraqis' suspicions of Americans, and the cultural ignorance of U.S. forces and policymakers. Second, the U.S. military must walk a fine line between risking the increased casualties that extended embedding of American soldiers in Iraqi units will produce and risking a collapse of recruitment and retention efforts that could result from a continued reliance on large U.S. troop deployments. Third, setting up effective Iraqi security forces will be a fitful, long-term process, and oil-spot operations could prove frustrating to a U.S. military that prefers to take the fight to the enemy through traditional offensive operations. Finally, coordinating and integrating security, intelligence, and reconstruction operations will require a level of U.S.-Iraqi cooperation and an integrated U.S. effort far beyond what the interagency process in Washington has produced—including strong central coordination and leadership from the senior political official on the scene, the U.S. ambassador to Baghdad.

Even if successful, this strategy will require at least a decade of commitment and hundreds of billions of dollars and will result in longer U.S. casualty rolls. But this is the price that the United States must pay if it is to achieve its worthy goals in Iraq. Are the American people and American soldiers willing to pay that price? Only by presenting them with a clear strategy for victory and a full understanding of the sacrifices required can the administration find out. And if Americans are not up to the task, Washington should accept that it must settle for a much more modest goal: leveraging its waning influence to outmaneuver the Iranians and the Syrians in creating an ally out of Iraq's next despot.

This article is part of the Foreign Affairs Iraq Retrospective.

The Price of the Surge

How U.S. Strategy Is Hastening Iraq's Demise

Steven Simon

In January 2007, President George W. Bush announced a new approach to the war in Iraq. At the time, sectarian and insurgent violence appeared to be spiraling out of control, and Democrats in Washington—newly in control of both houses of Congress—were demanding that the administration start winding down the war. Bush knew he needed to change course, but he refused to, as he put it, "give up the goal of winning." So rather than acquiesce to calls for withdrawal, he decided to ramp up U.S. efforts. With a "surge" in troops, a new emphasis on counterinsurgency strategy, and new commanders overseeing that strategy, Bush declared, the deteriorating situation could be turned around.

More than a year on, a growing conventional wisdom holds that the surge has paid off handsomely. U.S. casualties are down significantly from their peak in mid-2007, the level of violence in Iraq is lower than at any point since 2005, and Baghdad seems the safest it has been since the fall of Saddam Hussein's regime five years ago. Some backers of the surge even argue that the Iraqi civil war is over and that victory on Washington's terms is in sight—so long as the United States has the will to see its current efforts through to their conclusion.

STEVEN SIMON is Hasib J. Sabbagh Senior Fellow for Middle Eastern Studies at the Council on Foreign Relations. From 1994 to 1999, he served on the National Security Council in positions including Senior Director for Transnational Threats.

Unfortunately, such claims misconstrue the causes of the recent fall in violence and, more important, ignore a fatal flaw in the strategy. The surge has changed the situation not by itself but only in conjunction with several other developments: the grim successes of ethnic cleansing, the tactical quiescence of the Shiite militias, and a series of deals between U.S. forces and Sunni tribes that constitute a new bottom-up approach to pacifying Iraq. The problem is that this strategy to reduce violence is not linked to any sustainable plan for building a viable Iraqi state. If anything, it has made such an outcome less likely, by stoking the revanchist fantasies of Sunni Arab tribes and pitting them against the central government and against one another. In other words, the recent short-term gains have come at the expense of the long-term goal of a stable, unitary Iraq.

Despite the current lull in violence, Washington needs to shift from a unilateral bottom- up surge strategy to a policy that promotes, rather than undermines, Iraq's cohesion. That means establishing an effective multilateral process to spur top-down political reconciliation among the major Iraqi factions. And that, in turn, means stating firmly and clearly that most U.S. forces will be withdrawn from Iraq within two or three years. Otherwise, a strategy adopted for near-term advantage by a frustrated administration will only increase the likelihood of long-term debacle.

THE SURGE'S FALSE START

After the February 2006 bombing of the Askariya shrine in Samarra, the White House started to become increasingly concerned that there were too few U.S. troops in Iraq. A network of retired army officers led by Jack Keane, a former vice chief of staff of the U.S. Army, had been pushing from the outside for an increase in forces, and Senators John McCain (R-Ariz.) and Lindsey Graham (R-S.C.) kept up a drumbeat of criticism of what they saw as a lackluster military effort. The November 2006 congressional elections, which handed the House and the Senate to the Democrats, added to the sense that a new strategy was needed. In a December 2006 memo, Bush's national security adviser, Stephen Hadley, somewhat gingerly noted that the United

States might "need to fill the current four-brigade gap in Baghdad with coalition forces if reliable Iraqi forces are not identified."

On December 13, 2006, Bush met with the Joint Chiefs of Staff at the Pentagon to persuade them to allocate more troops to Iraq. It was not an easy sell. U.S. ground forces are not configured to fight such a long war, and the repeated deployment of the same active-duty and Reserve units had taken a toll. The reenlistment rate of young captains, for example, had fallen to an unprecedented low; about half of the West Point classes of 2000 and 2001 had decided against an army career. The pace of unit rotations and the tempo of operations had also taken their toll on equipment, which was wearing out at nine times the normal rate, faster than it could be replaced. The chairman of the Joint Chiefs of Staff made clear his concern about the army being stretched too thin. A shortfall of 10,000 company-grade officers meant that the Reserve units would have to rob both people and materiel from other units. Meanwhile, the mounting expense of the war was crowding out the procurement of new combat systems for the navy and the air force, and there was a growing risk that the military might find itself without the capacity to meet other strategic challenges, whether from Afghanistan, Iran, or elsewhere.

Bush tried to allay these worries, pledging to, among other things, increase the size of the U.S. Army and the Marine Corps and boost defense spending. But the Joint Chiefs also conditioned their reluctant support of the surge on a promise from the president to hold Iraqi Prime Minister Nouri al-Maliki's feet to the fire on political reconciliation. So when Bush unveiled his surge strategy in January 2007 (the deployment of an additional 21,500 troops, through September, with the initial military objective of restoring order to Baghdad), the stated purpose was to ensure that "the [Iraqi] government will have the breathing space it needs to make progress in other critical areas. Most of Iraq's Sunni and Shia want to live together in peace—and reducing the violence in Baghdad will help make reconciliation possible." Bush quoted Maliki's promise that the Baghdad security plan would "not provide a safe haven for any outlaws, regardless of their sectarian or political affiliation."

Even then, however, the administration was already starting to doubt Maliki's competence and willingness to pursue reconciliation, the principal determinant of long- term stability in Iraq. Two months earlier, Hadley had visited Iraq to assess the prospects for a cross-sectarian political rapprochement and come away unsure of Maliki's stance. "Do we and Prime Minister Maliki," Hadley had wondered in his December 2006 memo, "share the same vision for Iraq? If so, is he able to curb those who seek Shia hegemony or the reassertion of Sunni power? The answers to these questions are key in determining whether we have the right strategy in Iraq." Hadley proposed several ways to test Maliki's intentions and bolster his resolve, including initiatives to rejigger parliamentary support to free Maliki from his Shiite base linked to Muqtada al-Sadr and enable him to take conciliatory steps toward the Sunnis. The United States, however, lacked the influence necessary to put this approach into practice. Before long, events in Iraq revealed the answers to Hadley's questions: in both cases, a resounding no.

The deployment of the five new brigades proceeded more or less as planned, but from the start there was little headway made toward the broader goals of the surge, particularly reconciliation, as measured by the Iraqi government's inability to meet key benchmarks. The Constitutional Review Committee, which was charged with redressing Sunni grievances, made little progress, and there was no progress on de-Baathification reform, amnesty, provincial elections, or the implementation of oil legislation. The Sunni Iraqi Accordance Front had walked away from Maliki's cabinet, and Bush's reportedly regular calls to Maliki urging him to mobilize his government were ineffective. The Iraqi committees created to support the Baghdad security plan were left unfilled, and the three Iraqi brigades needed to help implement it arrived late and understrength. Diplomatic efforts to get Iraq's neighbors involved fizzled.

FROM TOP DOWN TO BOTTOM UP

The president's hopes for the top-down political efforts that were supposed to accompany the surge quickly faded. As a substitute, however, a new bottom-up strategy was embraced. Bush had observed in his January surge speech that the Sunnis were challenging al Qaeda's presence in Iraq, and a February 2007 National Intelligence Estimate on Iraq recommended "deputizing, resourcing, and working more directly with neighborhood watch groups and establishing grievance committees—to help mend frayed relationships between tribal and religious groups, which have been mobilized into communal warfare over the past three years." A few months later, the president signaled a formal shift in strategy in a speech at the Naval War College: "To evaluate how life is improving for the Iraqis, we cannot look at the country only from the top down. We need to go beyond the Green Zone and look at Iraq from bottom up. This is where political reconciliation matters the most, because it is where ordinary Iraqis are deciding whether to support new Iraq or to sit on the fence, uncertain about the country's future." What the president was proposing was a shift in the U.S. approach to counterinsurgency. Now, the United States would work to exploit a grass- roots anti-al Qaeda movement already under way by taking the pressure off the insurgents who had begun to point their weapons at the jihadists and funneling money to tribal leaders. In theory, this would help dismantle the jihadist infrastructure and create islands of stability that would eventually join up like "oil spots."

After the U.S. invasion, the Sunni groups that would go on to make up the insurgency arrived at a marriage of convenience with the foreign and local jihadists who made up al Qaeda in Iraq. The two shared a common goal: to reverse the triumph of the Shiites and restore the Sunnis to their lost position of power. For the Sunni insurgents, the presence of foreign jihadists also helped divert the attention of U.S. forces. Up to a point, therefore, al Qaeda's excesses—such as its attempt to impose strict Wahhabi- style rule by banning music and satellite dishes and compelling women to cover themselves entirely—were to be tolerated.

But for al Qaeda, the link with the insurgents was supposed to serve two additional purposes that went well beyond the shared goal of chipping away at Shiite predominance—and ultimately went against the interests of the Iraqi Sunnis themselves. The first was to establish an al Qaeda-dominated ministate as a base for carrying out jihad against enemies outside of Iraq. (The November 2005 attack against three Western tourist hotels in Amman, Jordan, allegedly ordered by Abu Musab al- Zarqawi, then the leader of al Qaeda in Iraq, was a harbinger of this wider strategy.) The second was to seize a leading position within the insurgency and thereby block a power-sharing arrangement between Baghdad and the Sunni nationalists, an arrangement that would entail the selling out of al Qaeda by the Sunnis.

The Iraqi Sunnis' enthusiasm for the alliance waned as al Qaeda increasingly attempted to assert its leadership. In October 2006, al Qaeda declared the formation of an Islamic state in Iraq, demanding that Sunni insurgent leaders pledge allegiance to the new (and many believed fictional) jihadist commander Abu Omar al-Baghdadi, whose name was supposed to signify an authentically Iraqi origin. To the nationalist insurgents, accepting the declaration of a separate state and ceding leadership to al Qaeda made little sense. Doing so would have fueled the process of decentralization, emboldened those Kurds and Shiites who sought their own fiefdoms, and, crucially, further distanced the Sunnis from eventual access to Iraq's potentially massive oil revenues. Moreover, despite the spectacular successes that had been attributed to al Qaeda, it was the nationalist Sunnis who provided the backbone of the insurgency and had done most of the killing and dying.

Some tribes had also grown increasingly resentful of al Qaeda's efforts to seize control of resources. The Albu Risha tribe, for example, had lost control over portions of the road from Baghdad to Amman, undermining its ability to raise revenue by taxing or extorting traders and travelers. When the Albu Rishas' leaders protested, the chieftain, Sheik Bazi al-Rishawi, was killed along with one of his sons, and two more of his sons were abducted. In response, Rishawi's fourth son, Sheik Abdul Sattar, assembled a small group of tribal figures (with the help of funds from the local U.S.

military commander) under the banner of the Anbar Salvation Council to roll back al Qaeda's influence. The bodies of al Qaeda personnel soon began turning up in alleyways.

This strategic schism might have been papered over had the jihadists not overreacted to the opposition of other insurgent groups. In 2007, there was a wave of sensational killings of Sunni leaders by al Qaeda, including Abdul Sattar (who had met with President Bush two weeks before his death). The assassinations of Sunni leaders warranted retaliation under the prevailing tribal code, opening the door to more systematic cooperation between the tribes and U.S. forces. In the wake of Abdul Sattar's death, a Sunni leader complained that al Qaeda's assassinations had "left resistance groups with two options: either to fight al Qaeda and negotiate with the Americans or fight the Americans and join the Islamic State of Iraq, which divides Iraq. Both options are bitter." After their defeat in the battle of Baghdad—thanks to the entrenched power of Sadr's Shiite Mahdi Army and the arrival of additional U.S. troops—the Iraqi Sunnis went decisively with the first option, marking the start of the Sunni Awakening groups. The United States, for its part, had its own incentive to cooperate with the insurgents: June 2007, with 126 troop deaths, was the second-worst month for the U.S. military in Iraq, and General David Petraeus, the U.S. ground commander, was facing pressure to reduce casualties quickly. The most efficient way to do so was to strike deals with the newly pliable insurgents.

The deals were mediated by tribal leaders and consisted of payments of $360 per month per combatant in exchange for allegiance and cooperation. Initially referred to by the United States as "concerned local citizens," the former insurgents are now known as the Sons of Iraq. The total number across Iraq is estimated at over 90,000. Although the insurgents turned allies generally come well armed, at least one unit leader, Abu al- Abd, commander of the Islamic Army in Iraq, who controls Sunni neighborhoods in Baghdad, has said that he receives weapons as well as logistical support from U.S. units. His arrangement is probably typical. In November 2007, he agreed to a three- month pact, open to extension.

This strategy has combined with other developments—especially the fact that so much ethnic cleansing has already occurred and that violence in civil wars tends to ebb and flow, as the contending sides work to consolidate gains and replenish losses—to bring about the current drop in violence. The Sunni sheiks, meanwhile, are getting rich from the surge. The United States has budgeted $150 million to pay Sunni tribal groups this year, and the sheiks take as much as 20 percent of every payment to a former insurgent—which means that commanding 200 fighters can be worth well over a hundred thousand dollars a year for a tribal chief. Although Washington hopes that Baghdad will eventually integrate most former insurgents into the Iraqi state security services, there are reasons to worry that the Sunni chiefs will not willingly give up what has become an extremely lucrative arrangement.

TRIBAL REALITIES

The surge may have brought transitory successes—although if the spate of attacks in February is any indication, the decrease in violence may already be over—but it has done so by stoking the three forces that have traditionally threatened the stability of Middle Eastern states: tribalism, warlordism, and sectarianism. States that have failed to control these forces have ultimately become ungovernable, and this is the fate for which the surge is preparing Iraq. A strategy intended to reduce casualties in the short term will ineluctably weaken the prospects for Iraq's cohesion over the long run.

Since the mid-nineteenth century, ruling powers in the Middle East have slowly and haltingly labored to bring tribal populations into the fold, with mixed success. Where tribes and tribalism have remained powerful, the state has remained weak. The Ottomans attempted forced sedentarization of the tribes, weakening tribal authorities by disrupting settlement patterns and replacing tribal sheiks with smaller cadres of favored leaders who became conduits for patronage. The colonial powers after World War I faced a different problem: the threat of nationalist urban elites opposed to foreign rule. In an effort to counter defiant urban leaders, they empowered rural tribes on the periphery. In Iraq, the British armed the tribes so that the sheiks could maintain order in the country-side and balance the capabilities of the nominal local governments operating under League of Nations mandates. Thus, the tribal system that Ottoman rule sought to dismantle was revitalized by British imperial policy, and the power of the nominal Iraqi government was systematically vitiated. In 1933, Iraq's King Faisal lamented, "In this kingdom, there are more than 100,000 rifles, whereas the government has only 15,000."

The tribes lost some power over the subsequent decades. This was in part a result of increasing direct British involvement in activities such as law enforcement, land tenure, and water distribution and in part a result of urbanization: as Iraqis moved from the country to the city, their affiliations shifted from the tribe to urban institutions—principally the trade union and the mosque—even as they held on to tribal symbols. When the Baathists took power in 1968, they explicitly rejected "religious sectarianism, racism, and tribalism . . . the remnants of colonialism." The tribes, in their minds, were inevitable rivals of a centralizing state. But after taking control in a coup in 1979, Saddam leaned on his own Sunni tribal networks to staff his security services, army leadership, and bureaucracy, while suppressing other tribal life. He tried to rein in tribes by dispersing Baathist apparatchiks throughout the hinter-land, but he nonetheless came to rely on the tribal system as a whole to make up for the shortcomings of the state as times became harder.

During the Iran-Iraq War, Saddam used Shiite tribes to defend regions near the Iranian border, and elsewhere tribal leaders regained some of their traditional authority as the war forced the redeployment of Baathist officials to the front. Amid the hardships created by the conflict, the flow of resources from the center shrank, leading to greater self-reliance in tribal areas and the renewed importance of tribal leaders. The Gulf War, and the grinding international sanctions that followed, accelerated these trends. In 1996, a high council of tribal chiefs was established and was granted political privilege, weapons, and land. Selected tribal leaders were allowed to enrich themselves by any means, fair or foul, and in return they were expected to defend the regime. Saddam, in effect, fostered a process of retribalization in Iraq.

Iraq's Arab neighbors, particularly Jordan and Saudi Arabia, provide a counterexample. They won enduring stability by corralling the tribes through a combination of reward and punishment. In Transjordan, King Abdullah I and the British—helped by famine and the effects of the Great Depression—confronted recalcitrant tribes militarily and then secured their allegiance with a steady flow of resources from the emerging state. More recently, Jordan's Hashemite monarchy has preserved the tribes' loyalty by guaranteeing them prestigious positions in the government and the military and by playing them off against the Palestinians. In Saudi Arabia, the al Saud dynasty consolidated its state by subduing the tribal challenge of rebellious Ikhwan and then endowing them with status and a military role. Strategic marriages between the al Saud family and the tribes cemented these ties. Although such efforts occasionally faltered, the thrust of the policy was always clear: to subordinate the tribes to the state.

Now, U.S. strategy is violating this principle by fostering the retribalization of Iraq all over again. In other countries in the region, such as Yemen, the result of allowing tribes to contest state authority is clear: a dysfunctional country prone to bouts of serious internecine violence. Such violence can also cross borders, especially if neighboring states are willing to use the tribes as their own agents. Pakistan provides a particularly ominous example of this dysfunctionality: its failure to absorb its Pashtun population has threatened the viability of the Pakistani state. The continued nurturing of tribalism in Iraq, in a way that sustains tribes in opposition to the central government rather than folding them into it, will bring about an Iraqi state that suffers from the same instability and violence as Yemen and Pakistan.

U.S. officials in Iraq have taken note of how the current U.S. approach has exacerbated the dangers of tribalism. Last month, a senior U.S. military adviser conceded, "We're not thinking through the impact of abetting further corruption and perpetuating tribal power." In December, a U.S. diplomat warned, "The absence of government in a lot of areas has allowed others to move in, whether militias or others." The net effect has been a splintering of the country rather than the creation of a unified nationalist Sunni front that, having regained its confidence, would be prepared to deal constructively with Baghdad.

THE CRUMBLING CENTER

The growth of warlordism is another consequence of the surge. By empowering the tribes and other networks without regulating their relationship to the state, the United States has enabled them to compete with one another for local control and what is mostly criminal revenue. It is worth noting that warlordism is not just a creeping Sunni phenomenon. Kurdish and Shiite criminals have been equally adept at exploiting the current security situation to their advantage. Indeed, warlordism appears even to be altering the sectarian divide. In Najaf, where gang warfare has erupted on more than one occasion, supporters of Sadr's Mahdi Army are engaged in street battles with members of the Badr Organization, even though both are Shiite groups.

Last December, a committee of British MPs charged with examining the security situation in Basra as British forces began to draw down concluded that warlords and criminal gangs had all but taken over the city. "Although the reduction in attacks on UK forces can only be welcome," the committee's report noted, "this alone cannot be a measure of success. The initial goal of UK forces in South Eastern Iraq was to establish the security necessary for the development of representative political institutions and for economic reconstruction. . . . This goal remains unfulfilled."

The United States' bottom-up strategy is also worsening sectarianism. For many Sunnis, reconciliation means restoration—not inclusion in power-sharing arrangements but regaining control of the state. Instead of discouraging this mindset, the evolution of the surge into a bottom-up operation has validated it, fostering the impression that Washington has at last recognized that its strategic interests lie with the Sunnis. As the Sunnis see it, the current U.S. strategy is a policy of organizing, arming, and training them to challenge Shiite supremacy.

The Shiites and the Kurds naturally have sharply different notions of what reconciliation means. For the Kurds, reconciliation means respect for their claims to autonomy as well as for their potential territorial gains. The Shiites have tended to emphasize the need for justice before reconciliation, which, as they see it, requires that they be compensated for their suffering under previous regimes (not only Saddam's). This, in their mind, necessitates the subordination of Iraq's Sunni population to the Shiite community. Some Shiite leaders have defied such thinking—Ayatollah Ali al-Sistani most prominently—but Sadr has made clear that he will use violence to secure Shiite hegemony, and Maliki's government has shown no willingness to be pried away from Sadr and like-minded Shiites. Indeed, in postconflict situations, reconciliation often founders on the unwillingness of victims to surrender their claims to justice.

Some Sunnis have started to recognize that the United States has no intention of restoring their supremacy. The realization that civilian jobs and vocational training is all that is in store for the 80 percent of the former insurgents who are blocked from membership in the Iraqi army (Shiite leaders want to dominate the army in order to use it as their own instrument of control) has eroded Sunni cooperation with U.S. forces. As one volunteer told a reporter, "The Sunnis were always the leaders of the country. Is it reasonable that they are turned into service workers and garbage collectors? . . . We had not anticipated this from the American forces. Of course we will not accept that." One response has been to head back to al Qaeda. An Awakening commander in the Diyala provincial capital of Baqubah, which has never been fully pacified, said in February, "Now there is no cooperation with the Americans. . . . We have stopped fighting al Qaeda." This was doubtless an exaggeration, but one that pointed to the hard truth that for many Sunnis, Shiite rule remains unacceptable. When former Sunni insurgents no longer believe that Washington will restore them to dominance, their current U.S. paymasters will once again be their targets.

Given the current trajectory, significant Sunni segments of the postsurge Iraqi state will continue to be funded by the United States, but they will remain beyond the control of either Baghdad or Washington. They will also be in a position to establish ties with neighboring countries. All of this may well accelerate the centrifugal forces unleashed by the bottom-up strategy. When it withdraws from Iraq, the United States will be leaving a country more divided than the one it invaded—thanks to a strategy that has systematically nourished domestic rivalries in order to maintain an illusory short-term stability.

This could mean that Iraq will remain essentially unreconstructed. The authority of the state would plummet, and the United States' ability to influence events, already limited, would become even weaker. Iraq would become a running sore, and successive crises within the country and on its borders would distract Washington from other priorities and sap its ability to normalize relations with Iran. For the Iraqis, safety, security, and economic advancement would remain uncertain. Those who could leave would. Stability would become an ever-receding prospect.

One plausible consequence of this turmoil would be the emergence of a U.S.-trained and U.S.-equipped Iraqi army, increasingly open to former officers of Saddam's military, as a powerful force in Iraqi politics. The professionalism and esprit de corps of the army is already on the rise. Officers who see themselves as having to navigate a maelstrom of unregulated militias, weak and irresponsible government officials, tribes emboldened and then embittered by their U.S. connections, and overbearing but uneven U.S. assertions of control could turn inward, as they did under the British and under Saddam. They might adopt a posture of superiority to politicians, impatience with upstart tribal leaders, and passive-aggressiveness toward their U.S. patrons and then sideline the civilian government and take control of the state. This result might be less disastrous than complete long-term breakdown: to the degree that Iraq needs a mediating military presence to sustain a fragile peace, this role might ultimately be better served by a military with its own corporate identity rather than by U.S. troops. But still, the United States would be confronted by a strong, centralized state ruled by a military junta that would resemble the Baathist regime Washington overthrew in 2003. Rather than an anarchic situation, the United States would face potentially aggressive nationalism and a regime unsympathetic to U.S. regional priorities.

RESPONSIBLE RETREAT

At this stage, the United States has no good option in Iraq. But the drawbacks and dangers of the current bottom-up approach demand a change of course. The only alternative is a return to a top-down strategy. To be more effective this time around, Washington must return to the kind of diplomacy that the Bush administration has largely neglected. Even with 160,000 troops in Iraq, Washington lacks the leverage on its own to push the Maliki government to take meaningful steps to accommodate Sunni concerns and thereby empower Sunni moderates. (The legislative package and the de-Baathification reform law passed earlier this year were seriously flawed and did more to spur the Sunnis' anxieties than redress their grievances.) What the United States could not do unilaterally, it must try to do with others, including neighboring countries, European allies, and the United Nations (UN).

In order to attain that kind of cooperation, Washington must make a public commitment to a phased withdrawal. Cooperation from surrounding countries and European partners is unlikely to be forthcoming without a corresponding U.S. readiness to cede a degree of the dubious control it now has over events in Iraq. Currently, the dominant U.S. presence in Iraq allows the rest of the world to avoid responsibility for stability in and around Iraq even as everyone realizes the stakes involved. A plan to draw down U.S.

forces would therefore contribute to the success of a larger diplomatic strategy, prompting Middle Eastern states, European governments, and the UN to be more constructive and proactive in working to salvage stability in the Persian Gulf.

The point, therefore, is not to focus on the precise speed and choreography of a troop withdrawal. Rather, what is necessary is to make clear that the United States intends to withdraw. Should the Bush administration suspend the currently programmed withdrawals of the surge force, it would send precisely the opposite message. President Bush, Secretary of Defense Robert Gates, and General Petraeus have all signaled their interest in halting any further drawdowns after the last surge brigade has come home this summer. Petraeus, who has already begun to lay out his case in interviews, argues that "the key is to hang on to what you've got." The president has suggested that he is unwilling to withdraw additional troops until after the Iraqi provincial elections—which, although originally scheduled for October, could very well be delayed. It is therefore possible that the next U.S. president will have to decide what to do with approximately 140,000 troops, a considerably larger number than most observers assumed would still be on the ground in Iraq at the end of 2008. (Some consideration will also have to be given to the problem of removing 56,000 contractors and facilitating the departure of a segment of the 30,000-50,000 Iraqi and foreign workers supporting the U.S. presence.)

Given that the laws of physics are as relevant to troop redeployments as are the laws of strategy and politics, the higher baseline bequeathed by Bush would mean a longer timeline for withdrawal. As of last summer, there were 1,900 tanks and other armored vehicles, 43,000 trucks, and 700 aircraft in Iraq. Equipment is scattered over 70 bases throughout the country, along with 38 major supply depots, 18 fuel-storage centers, and 10 ammunition dumps. According to the conservative rule of thumb used by military logisticians, the U.S. Army and the Marine Corps could move a brigade per month from the Iraqi theater. Moving the 15 brigades likely to be in Iraq in January 2009 would require up to 10,000 truck trips through potentially hostile zones within Iraq.

Although fixating on an exact timetable for withdrawal might be unhelpful at this juncture, a new administration should begin to draw down deliberately and in phases as soon as its internal deliberations are complete and the process has been coordinated with Baghdad. These steps could take months, as the new team conducts its policy- review process; military planners plot safe and efficient withdrawal routes; congressional consultations are carried out; conclusions are reached about where the forces being drawn down should be redeployed; planners determine the size, roles, and missions of the residual force; and the numerous dependencies created by the occupation and the surge are gradually shed. Once under way, however, a drawdown of most of the troops now in Iraq could be completed within two years. The redeployment might proceed more quickly if U.S. public support for the war collapsed, the Iraqi government demanded a swifter withdrawal, or the political situation in Iraq settled down; alternatively, the process might take more time if U.S. forces were under attack, an atrocity claiming the lives of many Americans occurred, or a responsible, reconciliation-minded Iraqi government and a concerned international community sought a slower drawdown.

RECONCILIATION FROM ABOVE

Announcing a withdrawal will entail certain risks. Aware that U.S. forces will finally be departing, Iraqi factions might begin to prepare for a new round of fighting. The Sunnis, aware of their vulnerabilities to attack by militant Shiite forces without the United States to protect them, might resuscitate their alliance with al Qaeda. The government in Baghdad might be concerned about its own exposure to attack in the absence of a U.S. shield and proceed to forge tighter links with Tehran or encourage greater activism by the Mahdi Army. It is all the more vital, therefore, that the drawdown take place as part of a comprehensive diplomatic strategy designed to limit these risks. The interval between a decision to withdraw and the removal of the bulk of U.S. forces should provide the space in which the UN can convene a multilateral organization to foster a reconciliation process in Iraq.

There is much that can be done to revitalize a top-down approach to reconciliation if it is under UN auspices and led by a credible special envoy. First, the international community should be energized to help Iraq move forward on provincial elections, which would test the popularity of the new Sunni leaders who have emerged during the surge and lash them up to Baghdad. This would have the added benefit of isolating the radical federalists from the majority of Shiites, who would prefer to live in a united Iraq. A UN envoy would have a better chance of brokering a deal on the distribution of provincial and federal powers, the issue that led to the veto of the provincial election law, than would Washington. In a multilateral setting that is not conspicuously stage- managed by the United States, regional states, including Iran and Saudi Arabia, could play a pivotal role in this process. Although Tehran's cooperation is inevitably hostage to its broader relations with Washington, UN sponsorship of this effort might provide the leaders of Iran with the cover they need to act in their own interest. The Saudis, for their part, would like to see the UN involved and are prepared to use their influence and money to impel the parties in Iraq toward reconciliation.

Second, an institutionalized multilateral group of concerned states should mobilize the broader international community to assist with the care, feeding, and permanent housing of the millions of refugees and internally displaced Iraqis who have not been able to get to the United States or Europe. This is essential, since refugee camps and squatter settlements are incubators of radicalism and radiate violence. The longer these populations remain unmoored and cut off from education, employment, and access to adequate social services and health care, the harder it will be to resettle them permanently, whether in Iraq or elsewhere.

Third, before a new and more intense phase of the civil war begins, there should be a multilateral process put in place to prod Saudi Arabia and other Persian Gulf states to finance investment projects that provide real employment in Iraq. Furthermore, Iraq's neighbors, including Iran, should be pressing the Iraqi government to bring far more Sunni Awakening volunteers into the regular Iraqi army and, crucially, into the provincial police forces funded by the central government. The latter step would reinforce the positive effects of the provincial elections and the emergence of politically legitimate local leaders. The current commitment to enlist 20 percent of the Awakening's members is far too small to have an impact.

Finally, the tribes feeding off the surge must be weaned from U.S. assistance and linked firmly to Baghdad as their source of support. Intertwining the tribes with Baghdad in this way, as the Iraq specialist Charles Tripp has noted, would yield something very much like the imperial protectorates in the Middle East of the first half of the twentieth century. The "club of patrons" in the capital would dole out goods to tribes through favored conduits. At this juncture, the U.S. military is performing the role of the patrons—creating an unhealthy dependency and driving a dangerous wedge between the tribes and the state. Through coordinated action by the UN sponsors of the multilateral process, the government in Baghdad, and U.S. commanders on the ground, payment responsibilities will have to be transferred from the U.S. military to Iraqi government representatives.

There is no guarantee that the old way of giving tribes a taste of the lash followed by a dollop of state largess—the model that successfully integrated tribes in Jordan and Saudi Arabia in the twentieth century—can be successfully applied to a divided Iraq today. Iraq is heterogeneous, unlike Jordan or Saudi Arabia, where the state and the tribes shared a religious heritage. Furthermore, overestimating Iranian or Saudi influence on Iraqi politics and the willingness of the UN Security Council to plunge into the existing morass is all too easy. In any event, it will be a slow and hazardous undertaking. Many things have to happen more or less simultaneously in a carefully coordinated chain of actions. Washington has to announce that it will begin withdrawing the bulk of its forces. The UN secretary-general, with the backing of the Security Council, must select a special envoy. A contact group of key states must be formed under UN sponsorship. Priorities and milestones will need to be set for the distribution of resources within Iraq, the recruitment of Sunnis to the army, provincial elections, foreign investment, dealing with refugees, and development assistance. Crucially, the phasing of the troop drawdown will have to mesh with this diplomatic process but not hinge on its ultimate success. This course is risky and possibly futile. Yet it is still a better bet than a fashionable, short-term fix divorced from any larger political vision for Iraq and the Middle East.

Listen to this essay: Download

This article is part of the Foreign Affairs Iraq Retrospective.

When to Leave Iraq

Today, Tomorrow, or Yesterday?

Colin H. Kahl and William E. Odom

WALK BEFORE RUNNING

Colin H. Kahl

In "The Price of the Surge" (May/June 2008), Steven Simon correctly observes that the Sunni turn against al Qaeda in Iraq (AQI), known as the Sunni Awakening, has been a key factor in security progress during the period of "the surge." Simon is also on point when he notes that the Awakening, which began before the surge, was not a direct consequence of additional U.S. troops. But although Simon gets much of the past right, he ultimately draws the wrong lessons for U.S. policy moving forward.

Rather than unilaterally and unconditionally withdrawing from Iraq and hoping that the international community will fill the void and push the Iraqis toward accommodation—a very unlikely scenario—the United States must embrace a policy of "conditional engagement." This approach would couple a phased redeployment of combat forces with a commitment to providing residual support for the Iraqi government if and only if it moves toward genuine reconciliation. Conditional engagement—rather than Simon's policy of unconditional disengagement—would incorporate the real lesson from the Sunni Awakening.

WILLIAM E. ODOM, a retired three-star General in the U.S. Army and former Director of the National Security Agency, is a Professor at Yale University and a Senior Adviser at the Center for Strategic and International Studies.

COLIN H. KAHL is an Assistant Professor in the Security Studies Program at Georgetown's Edmund A. Walsh School of Foreign Service and a Fellow at the Center for a New American Security.

The Awakening began in Anbar Province more than a year before the surge and took off in the summer and fall of 2006 in Ramadi and elsewhere, long before extra U.S. forces started flowing into Iraq in February and March of 2007. Throughout the war, enemy-of-my-enemy logic has driven Sunni decision-making. The Sunnis have seen three "occupiers" as threats: the United States, the Shiites (and their presumed Iranian patrons), and the foreigners and extremists in AQI. Crucial to the Awakening was the reordering of these threats.

When U.S. forces first arrived in Anbar, upending the Sunni-dominated social order, they were viewed as the principal threat. Because AQI fought the United States, it was seen by the tribes as a convenient short-term ally, despite deep distrust. This ordering of threats changed in 2005 and 2006. For one thing, U.S. forces became more effective and discriminating in their counterinsurgency activities. AQI, meanwhile, became more brutal and indiscriminate, forcing the tribes to start defending themselves. In the fall of 2006, it also declared the establishment of the Islamic State in Iraq, asserting political and economic hegemony over Anbar and other provinces with significant Sunni Arab populations. It started demanding brides, enforcing harsh fundamentalist social norms, and cutting into the tribes' smuggling revenues.

At the same time, U.S. forces had to convince the Sunnis that they were not occupiers—that is, that they did not intend to stay forever. Here, growing opposition to the war in the United States and the Democratic takeover of both houses of Congress in the November 2006 elections were critical. Major General John Allen, the Marine Corps officer responsible for tribal engagement in Anbar in 2007, recently told me that among Sunni leaders, the Democratic victory and the rising pro-withdrawal sentiment "did not go unnoticed. . . . They talked about it all the time." According to Allen, the marines, from top to bottom, reinforced the message sent by the Democratic takeover by saying, "We are leaving. . . . We don't know when we are leaving, but we don't have much time, so you [the Anbaris] better get after this." As a result, U.S. forces came to be seen as less of a threat than either AQI or the Shiite militias—and the risk that U.S. forces would leave pushed the Sunnis to cut a deal to protect their interests while they still could. As Major Niel Smith, the operations officer at the U.S. Army and Marine Corps Counterinsurgency Center, and Colonel Sean Mac-Farland, the commander of U.S. forces in Ramadi during the pivotal period of the Awakening, wrote recently in Military Review, "A growing concern that the U.S. would leave Iraq and leave the Sunnis defenseless against Al-Qaeda and Iranian-supported militias made these younger [tribal] leaders [who led the Awakening] open to our overtures." In short, contrary to the Bush administration's claims, the Awakening began before the surge and was driven in part by Democratic pressure to withdraw.

It was also critical, however, that U.S. forces did not leave immediately. According to Allen, the continued U.S. presence allowed U.S. commanders to argue that their troops would be the Sunnis' "shock absorbers" during the transition. In other words, the surge and the threat of withdrawal interacted synergistically: the threat of withdrawal made clear that the U.S. commitment was not open-ended, and the surge made clear that U.S. forces would be around for a while. Together they provided a strong incentive for the Anbaris to cooperate with the United States and turn on AQI.

This revised history of the Sunni Awakening has significant implications moving forward. Now, the principal impediment to long-term stability in Iraq is the reluctance of Prime Minister Nouri al-Maliki's central government to engage in genuine political accommodation. That will require a hydrocarbon law designed to equitably share oil revenues, better budget execution and service provision, steps to resettle and compensate victims of sectarian violence, resolution of the disputed status of Kirkuk, and efforts to demobilize and co-opt the Shiite militias (principally Muqtada al-Sadr's Mahdi Army). It will also require that the Shiite government integrate or otherwise employ the 90,000 "Sons of Iraq," mostly Sunni tribal militia members and former insurgents. After considerable cajoling, Maliki has agreed to integrate about

20 percent of the Sons of Iraq into the Iraqi army and police and provide the remainder with nonsecurity jobs. But his government has been very slow in carrying out this pledge, and the 20 percent figure is unlikely to be sufficient. Brigadier General Shija al-Adhami, the head of the Awakening force in Baghdad's Ghazaliya neighborhood, recently told The Washington Post, "This is a big failure—either they take us all in or this is not going to work."

Convincing the Iraqi government to make the tough decisions needed for accommodation requires following the same logic that drove the Awakening: using the risk of abandonment to generate a sense of urgency while committing to protecting groups that make tough choices. The Bush administration has thus far failed to generate the leverage such a strategy would produce because it has effectively given the Iraqi government a blank check. To the degree that minimal political progress has occurred, it can be attributed at least as much to the prospect that the Democrats in Congress might force a withdrawal as to overt threats from the Bush administration. Secretary of Defense Robert Gates admitted as much last April: "The debate in Congress . . . has been helpful in demonstrating to the Iraqis that American patience is limited. The strong feelings expressed in the Congress about the timetable probably has had a positive impact . . . in terms of communicating to the Iraqis that this is not an open-ended commitment."

As the United States moves forward in Iraq, more leverage is required, but the positions now being advanced by many Republicans and Democrats fail to offer the right mix of incentives to get the Iraqis to act. President George W. Bush has signaled his intent to "pause" the planned troop withdrawals when the surge ends, and Senator John McCain (R-Ariz.) speaks of staying in Iraq for a hundred years, no strings attached. This policy of unconditional engagement will not work, because there are no consequences for Iraq's leaders if they fail to accommodate one another. Some Democrats, on the other hand, side with Simon and are calling for a unilateral timetable for the complete withdrawal of all U.S. forces, regardless of the conditions on the ground. This policy of unconditional disengagement also gives up too much leverage, because it provides no ability to the Iraqi government to affect the pace of redeployment or the nature of U.S. support in exchange for making tough choices. Unconditional engagement is all carrots, no sticks; unconditional disengagement, all sticks, no carrots.

A new policy of conditional engagement would take advantage of the ongoing talks aimed at shaping a long-term U.S.-Iraqi security framework to push the Iraqis toward political accommodation. U.S. negotiators should exploit the continuing discontent among Democrats in Congress and the impending presidential election to signal that a long-term U.S. commitment to Iraq is not politically sustainable unless there is tangible evidence of reconciliation. Because the Iraqi government has an interest in a long-term security relationship with the United States, especially continued U.S. support for the Iraqi security forces, this tactic could prove very effective.

The presidential candidates from both parties should reinforce this strategy by publicly endorsing the conditions the Iraqi government must meet in order to influence the pace of future U.S. withdrawals and gain their future administrations' support for the Iraqi security forces in the years ahead. This will require the Democratic nominee to clarify his or her stance on the disposition of residual forces in Iraq after a withdrawal of most of the combat troops (only Senator Barack Obama [D-Ill.] has proposed explicit conditions to be placed on continued support for the Iraqi security forces), and it will require McCain to abandon his unconditional pledge to stay in Iraq.

When the new administration takes office in January 2009, it must follow up on this approach by initiating a down payment on redeployment. Starting from the roughly 15 combat brigades (a total of 130,000-140,000 troops) it is likely to inherit, the new administration should signal its intention to transition to a "support," or "overwatch," role by announcing the near-term reduction of U.S. forces to perhaps 12 brigades. The new administration should also immediately sign a formal pledge with the Iraqi government stating unequivocally that it will not seek, accept, or under any conditions establish permanent or "enduring" military bases in Iraq. Taken together, these actions would signal to the Iraqi government that the U.S. commitment is no longer open-ended while still maintaining enough forces in the near term to prevent a major reversal of progress on security. These steps would also signal to groups inside the Iraqi parliament that strongly oppose the occupation (especially the Sadrists), as well as to the organizations representing the nationalist wing of the Sunni insurgency, that the United States does not intend to stay forever. This might open up additional avenues for bringing those Sunnis into formal and informal negotiations.

Simultaneous with these decisions, the United States should start negotiations to establish a broad time horizon for the transition of the remaining U.S. forces to an overwatch role and the conditions for continued U.S. support for the Iraqi government. Once U.S. forces have reached a sustainable overwatch level, the primary mission of the U.S. military in Iraq will switch to counter-terrorism, training and advising of the Iraqi security forces, and force protection for U.S. civilians and advisers. U.S. negotiators should make clear, however, that continued economic and diplomatic support, as well as continued support for the Iraqi security forces (something the Iraqi government deeply desires and needs), will hinge on continued progress toward political accommodation. U.S. negotiators should emphasize that over the long run, the United States intends to normalize its relationship with the Iraqi government and redeploy all of its remaining forces as conditions permit. This policy of conditional engagement should be nested within a wider regional diplomatic initiative that seeks to leverage the U.S. drawdown in Iraq and the common interest among Iraq's neighbors in avoiding a failed Iraqi state.

In the end, this approach may not work. If the Iraqis prove unwilling to move toward accommodation, then no number of U.S. forces will be able to produce sustainable stability, and the strategic costs of maintaining a significant presence will outweigh the benefits. If so, the new administration should shift to Simon's unconditional disengagement as Plan B.

RUSH TO EXIT

William E. Odom

Simon provides a brilliant analysis of Iraq's political realities, past and present, exposing the effects of the U.S. occupation. Sadly, neither the administration nor all but a few outside analysts foresaw them. More recently, most media reporting has wholly ignored the political dynamics of the new "surge" tactic. And peripatetic experts in Washington regularly return from their brief visits to Iraq to assure the public that it is lowering violence but fail to explain why. They presume that progress toward political consolidation has also been occurring, or soon will be. Instead, as Simon explains, political regression has resulted, a "retribalization" of the same nature as that which both the British colonial rulers and the Baathist Party tried to overcome in order to create a modern state in Iraq.

This should hardly come as a surprise. The history of tribalism in Iraq is well known. When the United States replaced the British in the Middle East after World War II, it set "stability" above all other interests there, maintaining it through a regional balance of power. President Bush's invasion of Iraq broke radically with this half-century-old strategy. The prospects of success, as Simon shows, were worse than poor.

Until recently, the wisdom of this new strategy has not been challenged. Instead, just as happened with regard to the war in Vietnam, the mainstream discussion has focused on tactics, "nation building" through elections, and diplomacy aimed at reconciling irreconcilable Iraqi elites. As a result, the domestic dialogue has not been serious, not even in this magazine, until the appearance of Simon's analysis.

Serious discussion today must be about how to deal with the repercussions of the tragic error of the invasion. The key to thinking clearly about it is to give regional stability higher priority than some fantasy victory in Iraq. The first step toward restoring that stability is the complete withdrawal of U.S. forces from Iraq. Only then will promising next steps be possible. Simon moves in the direction of such an approach, although not far enough. He shows unambiguously why the United States must withdraw from Iraq, but his hesitant formula for withdrawal risks sustaining the paralysis U.S. strategy now suffers from and could make regional stability far more difficult to restore.

Fear of the chaos that a U.S. withdrawal would catalyze is the psychological block that prevents most observers from assessing the realities clearly. As such observers rightly claim, the United States will be blamed for this chaos, but they overlook the reality that the U.S. military presence now causes much of the chaos and has been doing so since 2003. The United States cannot prevent more chaos by remaining longer. Preventing it is simply not an option. The United States can, however, remove the cause of disorder by withdrawing its forces sooner rather than later. That is the only responsible option.

I was convinced that Simon understood this until he began speaking of "a top-down approach to reconciliation" to be implemented "under UN auspices and led by a credible special envoy." Why should a UN special envoy move into the U.S.-guarded Green Zone as long as insurgents and militias occasionally fire mortar rounds and rockets into it? Some sort of UN-led effort may eventually become possible, but it is not likely as long as U.S. forces remain. And even a UN envoy could not "reconcile" Iraq's warring factions "from the top down."

Simon does understand that the United States' departure will force other countries, especially in Europe, to reconsider their hands-off policies toward Iraq. It will also lead Iraq's neighbors to rethink their hands-on policies. They all want stability there, but some are meddling in ways that exacerbate instability. Once U.S. forces leave, instability may be even less in their interests. Thus, the faster U.S. forces depart, the greater the shifts in other countries' policies will be. A two-year schedule for removing U.S. forces, as Simon proposes, would fail to achieve most of this shock effect.

After recognizing the breakout potential of withdrawal, Simon effectively reembraces strategic paralysis. Otherwise, he would not insist that Iraq's tribal fragmentation must be overcome by means other than civil war and violence. He recognizes that U.S. legitimacy for sponsoring such an effort has been lost—if it ever existed—and so he wants to try a multilateral substitute involving the UN. Its prospects for success, however, are dubious in the extreme. If it consists only of Western countries, it will never be seen as legitimate, only as a Crusade in another form. If it includes countries from the region, they are unlikely to agree on fundamental issues about the kind of Iraq they will permit. Moreover, a UN entity's military component would prove far less effective in dealing with insurgents, militias, and the Ministry of Interior's death squads. Its weakness would invite violence, not reduce it. And neighboring countries would support militant resistance for their own interests.

Tribalism will not be subdued in a couple of years, or even a couple of decades. Two well-known British officials in the 1920s, fluent in Arabic and deeply knowledgeable about the Arabs, T. E. Lawrence and Gertrude Bell, slowly relinquished their hopes for such an outcome in Iraq. And the fragmentation there today is not just along tribal lines. The larger Sunni-Shiite sectarian divide, although often overemphasized, has been made far more serious as a result of the U.S. occupation and the holding of democratic elections before a political consolidation was achieved. Kurdish separatism is probably as strong as it has ever been. These divides are unlikely to be bridged by any means other than a civil war fought to a decisive conclusion. This reality indicates that Iraq's eventual rulers are not now in the Green Zone, and when they one day occupy the capital, all foreign elements will be gone. Association with U.S. forces contaminates any would-be Iraqi regime. A UN entity would not overcome that handicap; at best, it could only sustain political instability and abet conflict.

Simon also argues that logistical imperatives require at least two years for the withdrawal of U.S. forces. That is probably true if all U.S. weapons and materiel are to be removed, but much of it is not worth the costs of hauling it back to the United States. Vast numbers of trucks and other equipment withdrawn from Kuwait in 1991 have never been used again and have been left in costly storage to rust. At least a thousand five-ton trucks can be found stored in Italy today, unused yet costing money to retain. If the highest priority is given to the withdrawal of personnel, not materiel, the required time can be dramatically shortened.

Other factors favor speed. Retrograde movements in war are risky affairs. They must be made when one has lost the initiative or when one's own forces are poorly deployed, which means the opponent has the advantage. More time favors the opponent even more. More speed reduces his opportunities. Speed would also improve diplomacy abroad and boost public morale at home. In the very best circumstances, uncertainties abound during strategic withdrawals.

Most critical in the long run is recognizing that the primary U.S. strategic interest in this part of the world was and still is regional stability. That means subordinating the outcome in Iraq to the larger aim. Getting out of the paralysis in Iraq, chaotic or not, is the sine qua non of any sensible strategy for restoring regional stability.

Finally, some kind of rapprochement with Iran is essential. Regional stability from the 1950s to the fall of the shah in 1979 rested on three pillars: cooperative relations with Iran, moderate Arab states, and Israel. That arrangement served the strategic interests, if not always the tactical interests, of all parties. When the United States lost its footing in Iran, U.S. military requirements for maintaining the balance rose dramatically. That explains the rapid buildup and eventual creation of the Central Command during the Carter administration. The only way to reduce U.S. military requirements in the region is to restore the United States' diplomatic straddle between the region's two major conflicts—the Arab-Israeli conflict and the Persian-Arab conflict. The invasion of Iraq not only destroyed the balance but is now imposing additional military requirements on the United States that cannot be sustained indefinitely.

How to Leave a Stable Iraq

Building on Progress

Stephen Biddle, Michael E. O'Hanlon, and Kenneth M. Pollack

T
he Iraq war has become one of the most polarizing issues in American politics. Most Democrats, including Senator Barack Obama (D-Ill.), want large, early troop cuts; most Republicans, including Senator John McCain (R-Ariz.), want U.S. troops to stay until Iraq's stability is guaranteed. Years of bad news from the front have hardened these divisions along partisan lines and embittered many on both sides. Today, however, there is reason to believe that the debate over Iraq can change. A series of positive developments in the past year and a half offers hope that the desire of so many Americans to bring the troops home can be fulfilled without leaving Iraq in chaos. The right approach, in other words, can partly square Obama's goal of redeploying large numbers of U.S. forces sooner rather than later with McCain's goal of ensuring stability in Iraq.

If the prognosis in Iraq were hopelessly grim, it might make sense for the United States to threaten withdrawal, hold its breath, and

Stephen Biddle is a Senior Fellow at the Council on Foreign Relations.

Michael E. O'Hanlon and Kenneth M. Pollack are Senior Fellows at the Brookings Institution. This article is based in part on a research trip made to Iraq in May- June 2008 and written as part of the joint Saban Center at Brookings-Council on Foreign Relations project on U.S. policy toward the Middle East.

hope for the best. But the prognosis is now much more promising than it has been in years, making a threat of withdrawal far from necessary. With a degree of patience, the United States can build on a pattern of positive change in Iraq that offers it a chance to draw down troops soon without giving up hope for sustained stability.

The last 18 months have brought major changes in the underlying strategic calculus facing Iraq's main combatants—undermining the Sunni insurgency, weakening the Shiite militias, severely degrading al Qaeda in Iraq (AQI), strengthening the Iraqi security forces (ISF), and creating new, more positive political dynamics and incentives. But these developments have also brought new, if less acute, challenges to the fore—demanding corresponding changes in U.S. and Iraqi strategy. Simply staying the course will not work under the new conditions in Iraq.

Both to deal with the new problems and to guard against any revival of the old ones, any further troop drawdowns, now that the "surge" is over, should be modest until after Iraq gets through two big rounds of elections—in late 2008 at the provincial level and in late 2009 at the national level—which have the potential either to reinforce important gains or to reopen old wounds. But starting in 2010, if current trends continue, the United States may be able to start cutting back its troop presence substantially, possibly even halving the total U.S. commitment by sometime in 2011, without running excessive risks with the stability of Iraq and the wider Persian Gulf region.

HISTORY OF VIOLENCE

Most Americans have a mental image of Iraq that is defined by the chaos of 2006. But Iraq today is a very different place than it was two years ago. Overall violence is down at least 80 percent since the surge began, and ethno-sectarian violence—the kind that seemed to be sucking Iraq into all-out civil war in 2006—is down by over 90 percent. Through June, the number of violent civilian deaths has averaged about 700 a month in 2008, a lower rate than in any previous year of the war (with the possible exception of

2003). U.S. military deaths in Iraq have dropped from about 70 a month in early 2007 to about 25 a month now, and the death rate for the ISF has fallen by half, from 200 a month to about 100. Although refugees and internally displaced people are not yet returning home in large numbers, so few Iraqis are now being evicted that the net displacement rate is about zero.

Meanwhile, the three main culprits in the ethno-sectarian violence of 2006 have stood down and agreed to cease-fires or been crippled by military defeat. Sunni insurgents overwhelmingly switched sides over the course of 2007, signing on to cease-fires with the Iraqi state mostly through the Sons of Iraq program, which now includes over 100,000 participants, who provide local security in exchange for legitimacy and financial support. The Shiite militias, especially Muqtada al-Sadr's Mahdi Army (also know as Jaish al-Mahdi, or JAM), have seen their position undermined by a combination of Sunni realignment, U.S. and Iraqi military pressure, the increasing independence of splinter and rogue groups, and a backlash against their own parasitic exploitation of the civilians they were ostensibly defending. And the most violent actors—Iraq's extreme chauvinist Sunni groups and AQI—have been driven from most of western and central Iraq and are losing their remaining urban havens in the provinces of Diyala, Nineveh, and Salah ad Din thanks to a series of offensives by U.S. and Iraqi forces. AQI will surely continue to be able to precipitate occasional incidents of terrorist violence from these hideouts, but its ability to foment large-scale low-intensity warfare is now hugely diminished.

This remarkable change in Iraq's security situation results from the interaction of AQI's errors, the surge in U.S. troop levels, the growing capacities of the ISF, and the downstream consequences of all of this for the Shiite militias. AQI's first big mistake was bombing the Shiite Askariya shrine in Samarra in February 2006. The attack drew the Shiite militias (many of which had been merely defensive) into the civil war in force and on the offensive, and so began the battle of Baghdad—a yearlong wave of sectarian violence pitting Sunni insurgents and their AQI allies against JAM and its allies. At the time, Americans saw this wave of bloodshed as a disaster, and in terms of human life it clearly was. But it enabled a later wave of cease-fires by fundamentally changing the Sunnis' strategic calculus. The battle of Baghdad gave the Sunnis a clear view of what an all-out war would really mean, and they did not like what they saw. With U.S. forces playing no decisive role, the Shiite militias overwhelmed the Sunni combatants in neighborhood after neighborhood. By goading the Shiite militias into open warfare, AQI had triggered a head-to-head fight in which the Sunnis were decisively beaten by the Shiite forces they had assumed they could dominate.

AQI's second mistake was alienating its Sunni allies. AQI treated Sunnis it judged insufficiently devout or committed with unspeakable brutality and appropriated Sunni smuggling networks in Anbar Province for its own use, leaving tribal sheiks impoverished. Once the battle of Baghdad had demonstrated to the Sunnis that AQI could offer no real protection against the Shiites, these costs no longer seemed worth it. By late 2006, the Sunnis had realized that they faced defeat unless they found new allies—and they turned to the United States while they still could.

The surge, and especially its new emphasis on the provision of direct population security by U.S. forces, enabled the Sunnis to survive this realignment in the face of AQI's inevitable counterattacks. In Anbar, U.S. firepower, combined with a persistent troop presence and Sunni knowledge of whom and where to strike, essentially expelled AQI from the province. News of this "Anbar model" spread rapidly among disaffected Sunnis elsewhere. In just a few months, the result was a large-scale stand-down of the Sunni insurgency and the decimation of AQI throughout western and central Iraq.

Cease-fires with Sunnis in turn facilitated cease-fires with key Shiite militias. Sadr's JAM had originally arisen to defend Shiite civilians from Sunni violence. But as that violence waned and resentment of JAM militia thugs (many of whom seemed mostly concerned with extorting personal profit) grew, Shiite support for

JAM plummeted—especially since the U.S. military buildup in Baghdad and the cease-fires with the Sunnis gave the United States enough troop strength to offer the Shiites security without gangsterism. Sadr, his popularity declining and his control over his own fighters increasingly tenuous, chose to stand down rather than confront the strengthened U.S. force.

The net result of all this was a profound change in the underlying strategic calculus in Iraq—setting off a virtuous cycle in which decreasing sectarian violence weakens the hand of prospective sectarian warriors, which helps further reduce violence. From 2003 to 2006, the self-interest of the key internal actors lay in warfare. By the middle of 2007, the key players saw their interests as best served by peace.

It is worth noting that separation resulting from sectarian cleansing was not the chief cause of the reduction in violence, as some have claimed. Much of Iraq remains intermingled but increasingly peaceful. And whereas a cleansing argument implies that casualties should have gone down in Baghdad, for example, as mixed neighborhoods were cleansed, casualties actually went up consistently during the sectarian warfare of 2006. Cleansing may have reduced the violence somewhat in some places, but it was not the main cause.

AN ARMY OF ITS OWN

As the violence declined, two big changes in the Iraqi state took place—one military, one political. On the military side, the ISF have grown much more capable than they were in 2006. There are now some 559,000 security personnel, with about 230,000 in the Iraqi army alone, and those ranks are growing by at least 100,000 new soldiers and police a year. Some 55 percent of the units rank in the top two tiers of readiness, according to U.S. assessment methods, which have been improved to include evaluations of actual battlefield performance. (Even these units, however, still need significant coalition help in some areas, particularly for more complex operations.)

The size and competence of these Iraqi forces have allowed U.S. commanders to maintain population security even as U.S. troop strength has declined significantly since the surge. With more troops to cover the battlefield, whole Iraqi battalions can be pulled off the battlefield temporarily for training, further increasing their capabilities. At the same time, the United States has greatly expanded its advisory effort. The typical Iraqi division now has over 100 U.S. Army and Marine advisers, who stay with it even in battle, and Iraqi units are often teamed up with U.S. units of comparable or smaller size. The greater availability of troops enables many of these teams to begin deployments in quiet sectors, building both skills and working relationships before being sent to high-threat areas.

Just as important as the ISF's size and technical proficiency are the major changes that have taken place in the ISF's politics and leadership. Sectarian, corrupt, incompetent, and turncoat officers have been removed. Aggressive recruitment and new amnesty and de-Baathification ordinances have led to increases in both the number of Sunnis, especially in the officer corps, and the number of people with prior military experience in the forces. Now, about 80 percent of the Iraqi army's officers and 50 percent of its rank and file are veterans of Saddam Hussein's military, and one of the most capable units in the Iraqi army, the First Brigade of the First Infantry Division, is 60 percent Sunni.

The cooling of Iraq's underlying sectarian tensions has interacted synergistically with these efforts. In an ongoing ethnosectarian war, sectarian officers can be purged, but their replacements will face the same pressures, making real change difficult. With ethno-sectarian violence in remission, the replacements for purged sectarians are now much better able to resist militia pressure or political interference. There are still problematic elements in the ISF, and a renewal of ethno-sectarian violence would severely test allegiances. But declining ethno-sectarian violence enables sectarianism to be policed more quickly, consistently, and harshly than in the past. (A U.S. Special Forces officer who served as an advisory-team commander in 2007 and 2008 noted that collaboration with one of the militant sectarian groups was one of the few offenses that typically resulted in an officer's dismissal or imprisonment.) The net result has been important progress, which has been reflected in improved public perception of the ISF: the percentage of Iraqis who did not believe that the Iraqi army was sectarian, according to polling conducted by the U.S.-led coalition, jumped from 39 percent in June 2007 to 54 percent in June 2008.

The Iraqi National Police provides another critical example of this progress. As recently as the fall of 2006, the national police force was a disaster; a commission led by retired Marine General James Jones went so far as to recommend its dissolution. It was infested with Shiite militias as well as every variety of coward and criminal, and police units often acted as anti-Sunni hit squads. But a new commander, Major General Hussein al- Wadi, has turned the force around. He fired both division commanders, all eight brigade commanders, and 18 of 27 battalion commanders. He instituted new vetting and screening measures, enrolled every member of his forces in the massive biometric data system, recruited Sunnis and Kurds into the force, and retrained every police formation. Today, the national police officer corps has roughly equal numbers of Sunnis and Shiites, and its rank and file is 25 percent Sunni— higher than the Sunnis' share of the overall population. Police units are now capable of supporting army units in combat zones, and popular trust in the police is growing. According to coalition polling, the percentage of Iraqis who believed that the Iraqi police were sectarian fell from 64 percent in June 2007 to 52 percent a year later, and the percentage who believed they were corrupt fell from 63 percent to 50 percent.

Despite such steps, the Iraqis are not yet able to stand on their own. They remain dependent on U.S. and British troops to assist with planning and provide logistical and fire support. (The "tooth-to-tail ratio" for the Iraqi army—the ratio of combat to support troops—is 75-25, the reverse of what it is for the U.S. Army.) Properly advised and partnered Iraqi formations perform far better than units without such support. In the offensive against JAM in Basra this past spring, for instance, the First Brigade and the 26th Brigade, which had long fought with U.S. marines and were deployed with Marine advisers, performed well, whereas the brigades without U.S. advisers and partners did poorly, with one, the new 52nd Brigade, effectively collapsing in combat. The Basra campaign would have ended in disaster if not for support from coalition firepower and the arrival of ISF units with U.S. military- and police-training teams. In short, the ISF have improved to the point where they have become a powerful partner to U.S. and coalition forces in Iraq, but they will require outside support for at least some time to come.

THE EMERGING POLITICS OF IRAQ

Iraqi politics are changing as well. Tensions, mistrust, and competitive pressures remain severe. But thanks to reduced violence, diminished sectarian warfare, weakened militias, and the prospect of upcoming elections for which Sunnis and others who boycotted the last round are expected to turn out in force, the old patterns of Iraqi political life are giving way to new ones. This moment of change brings risk and uncertainty, but those old patterns were so clearly dysfunctional that this transition offers an important opportunity.

During the years of severe ethno-sectarian violence, the three most influential political entities in Iraq—the Islamic Supreme Council of Iraq, the Sadrist movement, and the Fadhila Party, all three of which are Shiite—owed their influence to their powerful militias, which could provide protection to those who needed it and intimidate those who did not. But over the past 18 months, these militias have been significantly weakened. The Islamic Supreme Council of Iraq's Badr Corps and Fadhila's militia have been integrating into the ISF for years. Today, they have largely vanished as independent militias using violence to advance their own political agendas and undermine central government rule. Meanwhile, JAM cadres, increasingly rejected by the Shiite population, which has come to see them more and more as members of predatory criminal gangs rather than as a necessary defense against Sunni attacks, have been routed on the battlefield or driven underground or into Iran. Communities once dependent on JAM now welcome ISF units as sources of law and order.

Sadr himself remains a popular figure among Iraq's downtrodden Shiite communities, if only because of his family ties and perceived nationalism. But he appears increasingly out of step with his erstwhile constituents. His long sojourn in Iran has removed him from day-to-day management of his movement and weakened his nationalist credentials. Sadr's calls for protests against the government now draw only a few thousand people out onto the streets, in contrast to the massive crowds he could bring out in the past. JAM cadres are increasingly frustrated with Sadr's lack of leadership. And U.S. officials report that more and more Sadrist officials have begun meeting with them in defiance of Sadr's orders. The Sadrist movement may be able to regroup—especially if the government fails to provide services and jobs, which JAM has sought to offer its supporters—but it is much weaker than it once was.

For their part, the Sunnis seem not only willing but also determined to participate in the government of Iraq, in ways they have not up to now. Most Sunni leaders have concluded that boycotting the 2005 elections was a mistake, which ended up ceding to the worst of the Shiite militias complete control of the central government and many provincial governments. Now, they are determined to participate: in the 2008 provincial elections in order to regain control over the governments of their provinces, and in the 2009 parliamentary elections in the hope of either taking part in a new government or at least preventing their rivals from depriving them of their fair share of Iraq's riches (now flowing from Baghdad to the provinces much more than before but still not enough). In many places, Sunni tribal leaders will try to supplant incumbents from existing Sunni political movements, many of whom are not particularly popular.

Now that the Iraqi people are rejecting the militias, the parties that had long served as façades for them are scrambling to be seen as helping to improve the government's capacity to deliver security and essential services, in the hope that voters will forget how badly the parties hindered that process before 2007. (Most of the established political parties are afraid of losing big in the coming elections, as voters turn to different leaders in an attempt to spur change.) The result has been a series of important political compromises among Iraq's senior leaders: in December 2007 and February 2008, they passed a budget law, a new de-Baathification law, an amnesty for former insurgents, a pensions law, and a provincial powers act that is an important part of an ongoing decentralization process.

Together, all of these developments raise the potential of creating a new and better political order in Iraq. For now, there is still more potential than realization. Legislative progress on reconciliation continues to be slow, factional and sectarian differences remain divisive, and there is still no new political alignment or movement with the power to bridge these divides. Moreover, elections have had a very mixed track record in Iraq: as in many emerging democracies, electoral incentives can lead to instability as well as progress. But recent changes in Iraq's underlying military and political dynamics have at least broken the pattern of dysfunctional politics that has paralyzed Iraq in recent years. And this creates an opening that, if the Iraqis and the Americans can exploit it, could lead to a very different pattern—one of positive political development and compromise.

Some argue that to do this, the United States must withdraw, or threaten to withdraw, its troops. They believe this would force Iraqi leaders to put their differences aside and reach a grand compromise on reconciliation, because Iraqis would need to solve their own problems either without a U.S. military crutch or in order to preserve a U.S. presence as a reward for reconciliation. There is some merit to this logic. It is true that the presence of U.S. forces reduces the stakes for Iraqi politicians, since it limits violence. And if Iraq faced chaos otherwise, a threat of withdrawal would certainly be worth trying. But withdrawal is a risky gambit. And progress is now being made without it: violence is down dramatically, and political change, although slow, is under way. Threatening withdrawal might speed this progress, but today it seems more likely to derail it instead.

Reconciliation will require all the major Iraqi factions to accept painful compromises simultaneously. If any major party holds out and decides to fight rather than accept risky sacrifices for the larger good, then its rivals will find it very hard to hold their own followers to the terms of a cease-fire—likely plunging Iraq back into open warfare. If reconciliation can be done slowly, via small steps, then each stage of compromise is likely to be tolerable, with the risk of one holdout party exploiting the others kept to a manageable level. In contrast, if reconciliation must be done quickly, with a grand bargain rapidly negotiated in the face of an imminent U.S. withdrawal, the necessary compromises will be great—making them extremely risky for all parties. In a factionalized, poorly institutionalized, immature political system such as Iraq's, many parties would doubt their rivals' motives and could refuse to make such large and risky compromises. The Iraqis, out of fear for their own safety, might well respond to a threatened U.S. withdrawal by preparing for renewed warfare. Rather than persuading the Iraqis to accept huge risks together, a threat of withdrawal would more likely produce the opposite effect.

Leverage to encourage compromise is important, as advocates of withdrawal argue, and U.S. policy has up to now erred in rejecting conditionality for U.S. aid and cooperation. But threatening withdrawal is hardly the only or the best way of gaining such leverage. Any element of U.S. policy can be made conditional—economic assistance, military aid, the U.S. position in negotiations over the legal status of U.S. forces—by offering benefits only in exchange for Iraqi cooperation. Withdrawal is the biggest potential threat that Washington can issue, but it is also a blunt instrument with great potential to damage both parties' interests. In an environment of increasing stability, the United States can now hope to succeed with subtler methods.

NEW PROBLEMS, NOT NO PROBLEMS

If the United States and its coalition partners are to keep Iraq moving toward stability, they must still overcome a range of new challenges. These problems promise to be generally less daunting than those faced at the beginning of 2007, but they could still plunge Iraq back into civil war. Iraq may no longer be a failed state, but it is certainly, as Emma Sky, chief political adviser to the U.S. military leadership in Iraq, puts it, a "fragile state," one that must become much stronger if it is to stand on its own and not fall back into chaos and war. Achieving this will require tackling a number of second- order issues, which are growing in visibility as the first-order problems of rampant sectarian and insurgent violence abate. There are a great many such second-order problems, but it is worth highlighting some of the most important.

First, there is the challenge of integrating the Sons of Iraq into the ISF and the Iraqi government. The stand-down of the Sunni insurgency under the Sons of Iraq program has been a critical element in the reduction in violence. The program has not "armed the Sunnis" for renewed warfare, as American critics have often claimed—the Sons of Iraq hardly lacked weapons when they were fighting as insurgents, and they have received none from the United States. The real problem is different. Most Sons of Iraq groups want to be integrated into the government security forces—a move they see as the best guarantee that a Shiite regime will not use the ISF to tyrannize them. But Prime Minister Nouri al-Maliki's government has been dragging its feet, out of fear of empowering Sunni rivals. Some mix of security-sector and civilian employment must be found for the Sons of Iraq to satisfy their economic needs—and their security concerns vis-à-vis Iraq's Shiite majority. As with other needed intersectarian compromises in Iraq, this will require hard bargaining. But the increasing stability, along with the security that the improving ISF give to the Maliki regime, offers a reason to believe that such bargaining can eventually succeed if the United States stands firm.

The Sons of Iraq system is also highly decentralized, with over 200 separate groups under contract. Many are wary and distrustful of rivals, as are most Iraqis. Violations of cease-fire terms and contract provisions are inevitable with so many actors and so much tension; active enforcement of the terms is therefore essential to keep the peace. This is typical of the early years of negotiated settlements to civil wars, which commonly require outside peacekeepers to stabilize cease-fires. Until the Sunnis fully trust the ISF, this role will largely fall to the U.S. military—and, in fact, many U.S. brigades already spend much of their time involved in peacekeeping duties to enforce the terms of Sons of Iraq contracts. This cease-fire policing function is likely to be an increasingly important mission for U.S. forces in Iraq.

Returning refugees and internally displaced people are another important second-order problem. The first-order problem of the civil war created about four million refugees and internally displaced people. Some of them are now starting to return home, and many more can be expected to follow if security continues to improve. The returnees often have neither jobs nor homes to return to. Although trying to put every family back in its original home would be simply impossible—in many cases, the homes of returning refugees or displaced people are occupied by others whose homes were destroyed—there need to be large-scale resettlement programs for the displaced. One solution would be a government voucher program to help people build new houses, perhaps in their original provinces but not necessarily their original cities or neighborhoods. Iraq should fund most of any such program, but American and international advisers can help design the program—and then help in the critical tasks of implementing it fairly across sectarian lines and protecting the populations trying to relocate. This approach would have the added virtue of sparking a construction boom and thereby helping reduce unemployment (one of Iraq's chief economic problems). Without such measures, considerable violence—both by and against the returnees—could ensue, perhaps resurrecting the militias as the champions of the dispossessed.

The Iraqi central government's administrative capacity and the country's economic progress still lag far behind the gains in security, and there is still much to be done before Iraq has a mature political system and a productive economy capable of meeting the Iraqi people's basic needs. The Iraqi government has proved unable to spend more than a modest fraction of its own revenue, leaving the Iraqis largely unable to benefit from record-high oil prices. Unemployment is between 30 and 40 percent, and there has been little documented progress in providing health care, education, sanitation, clean water, or most other services. Money and goods are finally moving across the country, but they are moving very slowly. Without an electronic banking system, it is difficult to transfer funds from the central government to the provinces, where they can be more effectively spent.

Credible public administration is important for sustaining improved security. Some recent policy changes are steps in the right direction. As part of the surge strategy, the United States increased its support to Iraq's provincial governments, which are better able than the central government to develop the capacity to deliver essential services. U.S. civilian and military personnel, most deployed in new Provincial Reconstruction Teams (PRTs) and Embedded Provincial Reconstruction Teams (EPRTs), have fanned out into the countryside to help Iraqi officials build local and provincial governance structures and utilities. Training programs for civil servants from provincial governments were established in Baghdad and Erbil to complement the work of the teams in the field. Likewise, the United States' economic-assistance strategy has shifted from an emphasis on massive U.S.-directed and U.S.-designed infrastructure programs to more effective local initiatives, such as microloans administered by the PRTs and the EPRTs (which are now nearly fully staffed).

There are signs that things are starting to improve on the economic front. U.S., Iraqi, British, and UN officials all say that there are more markets opening up, more businesses starting or reopening, and more traffic on the streets than in the past few years. In an area of Iraq south of Baghdad once so violent that it was known as "the Triangle of Death," 255 small businesses were opened in the first five months of 2008. Still, on economic issues, the glass remains less than half full, and the delivery of essential government services remains an important challenge.

A final second-order problem worth noting is the thorny issue of Kirkuk. Preventing Kirkuk from becoming a flashpoint will require compromises on a range of difficult issues. The city and its environs, once heavily Kurdish, were "Arabized" by Saddam in an effort to weaken the Kurdish hold on Iraq's northern oil-producing region. Many Kurds were displaced by the influx of Arabs, and now, in much of the city, two different families claim every house. A solution might involve giving most Kurds their homes back or creating a voucher system to enable them to build new ones. Ensuring that all of Iraq's major groups are comfortable with a settlement on oil-revenue sharing and oil exploration will also be critical for Kirkuk. A fair resolution on oil requires making future oil wealth a national asset to be shared equally by all Iraqis. Resolving the problem of Kirkuk is likely to take considerable time, especially since any rapid resolution might produce considerable bloodshed. But the good news is that the Kurdish leadership recognizes the difficulties inherent in amicably resolving the Kirkuk problem and has so far supported the UN process established to handle it.

THE PROBLEM WITH POLITICS AS USUAL

As Iraq moves toward stability, other problems will start to emerge. Iraq risks becoming an ordinary Arab state—hardly a rosy prospect given the horrendous political and economic record of other Arab states in the region over the past 60 years. As the United States and its partners work on such basic challenges as resettling refugees and improving government capacity, they must also try to prevent the fragile new Iraq from falling prey to the kinds of problems that have befallen so many other Arab states.

The most pressing risk is that the much-improved ISF, an increasingly competent and self-confident institution in a state of otherwise weak institutions, could turn to praetorianism. Even a failed coup attempt could have serious consequences, rekindling sectarian rivalries and causing the ISF themselves to fragment along sectarian lines. The United States' continued military presence can be an important deterrent in this regard; a rapid U.S. withdrawal could greatly increase the risk of a coup.

It is also possible that a clique of politicians aligned with the security services could take over the government from within and then proceed to hoard its vast energy wealth and parcel out the rest of the state to organized crime. The ties between increasingly prevalent organized crime and many Iraqi political leaders, the stronger ISF at their disposal, and Iraq's oil wealth make this a very real danger. Still another possibility would be Iraq's falling into a "Palestinian model," in which the central government fails to provide essential services and steals the country's wealth. That could create fertile ground for Hamas-like militias to provide many services (as JAM was attempting to do before the ISF displaced it).

None of these outcomes would bring sustainable stability to Iraq, and all would risk reigniting the civil war. The second-order problems thus demand increasing attention as the first-order problem of ethno-sectarian violence ebbs.

The United States must also contend with Iran's role. The war in Iraq is ultimately about Iraq and the Iraqis, but Iranian money, weapons, and training for Iraqi militias and guerrillas are clearly exacerbating Iraq's internal problems. How committed Iran is to this policy of malign interference, however, is unclear. The Iranian leadership is not entirely of one mind regarding its goals or strategies in Iraq, and the events of the past year and a half (particularly the weakening of the Shiite militias) appear to have shattered whatever consensus it once had. Iran has also done some things that could be beneficial—such as trying to prevent fighting among the Shiite militias—and the fact that it has done them to serve its own interests should not blind the United States to Iran's potential to be helpful in some regards.

Handling Iran will require a joint U.S.-Iraqi effort to engage Iran in a dialogue, in the hope of making Tehran more of a partner in the reconstruction effort. The Iranians need to be encouraged to do more of what is helpful and less of what is unhelpful, and the best route to that is to stop trying to exclude them from the process altogether. For instance, the U.S. and Iraqi governments should offer the Iranians a permanent liaison presence in Baghdad and other Iraqi cities, allowing them to be briefed and to offer advice on developments relevant to their interests. Better still would be to act where possible in ways that take Iran's advice into account to reassure Tehran that it can secure its most basic interests without having to fight for them. Even a failed attempt at dialogue would underscore to the Iraqis that Iran is acting nefariously in their country—making the Iraqis more tolerant of decisive government action against Iranian- sponsored militias and encouraging Iraqi, rather than U.S., action against Iranian arms smuggling and other types of interference.

WHITHER THE U.S. PRESENCE?

For now, U.S. troops are playing an important role in sustaining the fragile hope and security in Iraq. But current troop levels cannot be maintained forever. How soon and how deep can a drawdown be without undermining the prospects for stability?

Exact projections of troop requirements are difficult to make, but current trends suggest that the United States should be able to cut its presence in Iraq substantially—perhaps by half—over the course of 2010 and 2011. Doing so would be contingent on making further progress against the insurgency, keeping the peace during the upcoming provincial and parliamentary elections, and continuing to assist the Iraqis as they work toward healing their sectarian divisions. A destabilizing election, a renewal of sectarian violence sparked by badly handed refugee returns or poor resolution of the Kirkuk dispute, or more destabilizing activity by Iran would change this timing. Any schedule for withdrawal will be subject to the inherent uncertainty of a conflict as complex as the one in Iraq.

Still, one possible model if current trends continue is provided by the recent developments in Anbar Province, which has famously gone from being the worst area of the country in 2006 to nearly its best today. In 2007, the United States had 15 maneuver battalions in the province; today it has only six. Now, U.S. marines participate in less than half of all patrols, and their aim is to drop that down to only 25 percent soon. Several hundred marines remain to advise the two Iraqi army divisions in Anbar, and a sizable number of Americans are working with the Iraqi police there. They will remain necessary for some time, as will further U.S. support of efforts to patrol Anbar's border with Syria to keep out foreign terrorists (who continue to enter Iraq at the rate of about 30 a month, down by two-thirds from earlier estimates but still a worrying figure). The United States will also have to continue to provide key "combat enablers"—aerial surveillance and air, artillery, and armor support—to Iraqi forces in battle. But the ISF are now providing most of the infantry and policing manpower in Anbar themselves, and U.S. forces there will soon be less than half the size they were in 2007, without any increase in violence or instability.

Another potential insight, despite the imperfect analogy, comes from the U.S. experience in Bosnia and Kosovo. A key to stability in the Balkans has been the continued presence of outside peacekeepers to enforce the deals that ended the fighting—much like U.S. forces are now doing in Iraq (but were not before). Within four years of the cease-fires in Bosnia and Kosovo, peacekeeping forces in both places had been reduced by about half without causing any resumption of violence. And over the succeeding years, the foreign troop presence fell even further, with a token force of less than ten percent of its original strength remaining in Bosnia today.

Drawdowns on this scale in Iraq cannot be rushed without serious risk. For now, a substantial U.S. presence is essential to stabilize a system of local cease-fires and maintain an environment in which gradual compromise can proceed without gambling on a single grand bargain among wary rivals in Baghdad. This is not to say that today's troop count can or should be maintained until

2010—modest near-term withdrawals to below the pre-surge levels will be necessary to establish a sustainable posture. The 130,000 troops and 15 brigades of the pre-2007 force may be too large to maintain into 2009 without unacceptable damage to the U.S. Army and the Marine Corps. But if the United States can maintain a substantial force in Iraq through the critical period of the next two to three years, there is now a credible basis for believing that major drawdowns after that can be enabled by success rather than mandated by failure.

Of course, much could still go wrong. And if an electoral crisis or some other event returns Iraq to civil war, it would be very hard to justify another troop surge to try to stabilize Iraq. Containment—withdrawing all U.S. troops while working to prevent the chaos in Iraq from spilling over to the rest of the region—would then become the United States' only realistic option.

But today, there is a real chance that U.S. persistence in the short term can secure a stable Iraq and enable major withdrawals in 2010 and 2011 without undermining that stability. The American people—to say nothing of the servicemen and servicewomen who are fighting—have every right to be tired of this war and to question whether it should have ever been fought. But understandable frustration with past mistakes, sorrow over lives lost, anger at resources wasted, and fatigue with a war that has at times seemed endless must not blind Americans to the major change of the last 18 months. The developments of 2007 and 2008 have created new possibilities. If the United States is willing to seize them, it could yet emerge from Mesopotamia with something that may still fall well short of Eden on the Euphrates but that prevents the horrors of all-out civil war, avoids the danger of a wider war, and yields a stability that endures as Americans come home.

Iraq, From Surge to Sovereignty

Winding Down the War in Iraq

Emma Sky

By September 2008, when General Raymond Odierno replaced General David Petraeus as the top commander of the Multi-National Force-Iraq, there was a prevalent sense among Americans that the surge of additional U.S. forces into the country in 2007 had succeeded. With violence greatly reduced, the Iraq war seemed to be over. In July 2008, U.S. President George W. Bush had announced that violence in Iraq had decreased "to its lowest level since the spring of 2004" and that a significant reason for this sustained progress was "the success of the surge."

The surge capitalized on intra-Shiite and intra-Sunni struggles to help decrease violence, which created the context for the withdrawal of U.S. forces from Iraq. With U.S. troops on pace to depart entirely by December 2011, Iraqis held successful national elections last March and, after nine months of wrangling, eventually formed a broadly inclusive government in December 2010. But Odierno—for whom I served as chief political adviser—understood that the surge had not eliminated the root causes of conflict in Iraq. As we realized then, the Iraqis must still develop the necessary institutions to manage competition for power and resources peacefully. Iraqi elites across the political spectrum felt that the Obama administration was

EMMA SKY served as Chief Political Adviser to General Raymond Odierno, Commanding General of the Multi- National Force-Iraq from 2008 to 2010.

focused more heavily on leaving Iraq than on supporting the country's attempt to build a democratic system of government. The withdrawal of U.S. forces from Iraq should mark an evolution in the U.S.-Iraqi relationship, not Washington's disengagement. Without continued U.S. support, there is a real danger that Iraq may not succeed in using the opening provided by the surge to strengthen its stability and achieve its democratic aspirations.

ONE LAST TRY

By the end of 2006, Iraq appeared to be teetering on the edge of civil war. Tens of thousands of Iraqis had fled their homes, and Baghdad had degenerated into armed sectarian enclaves. Insurgent groups, criminal gangs, and militias of political parties used violence to achieve their particular objectives. Neighboring countries backed them with funding, paramilitary training, and weapons, further fomenting instability. Meanwhile, back in the United States, public support for the war was waning. The prevailing U.S. strategy of attempting to transfer responsibility for security to the Iraqi security forces (ISF) seemed, in the words of U.S. Army Colonel H. R. McMaster, "a rush to failure."

The question became whether the United States would leave Iraq as quickly as possible or attempt to implement a new strategy to reduce the violence—raising U.S. troop levels and employing different tactics. Joe Biden, who was then a U.S. senator, adamantly opposed such a troop buildup, arguing in early 2007 that "a surge of up to 30,000 American troops cannot have any positive effect except for only temporary." Yet Bush, U.S. Senator John McCain, and others believed that a troop surge could provide enough security against sectarian violence to allow for political reconciliation. They were convinced that a withdrawal of forces under such circumstances would cause an all-out civil war that could spread into neighboring countries, jeopardizing oil exports across the region. Proponents of a surge also believed that abandoning Iraq would gravely harm the global reputation of the United States, boost the morale of Islamic extremists, and crush the spirit of the U.S. military.

In a televised address in January 2007, Bush announced that the United States would implement a surge of U.S. forces "to help Iraqis carry out their campaign to put down sectarian violence." Petraeus—who became commanding general of the Multi-National Force-Iraq in January 2007—and Odierno, who was his second-in-command, shared responsibility for developing the new strategy on the ground. Serving as operational commander, Odierno proposed sending U.S. troops out into Iraqi population centers to protect civilians. This marked a break from the previous U.S. approach, which had U.S. troops targeting insurgents from bases on the outskirts of Iraqi cities and then quickly withdrawing, leaving the unreliable ISF in their place. Additional U.S. forces were sent to the Sunni-dominated Anbar region—an erstwhile stronghold of al Qaeda whose tribes were beginning to abandon the terrorist group and ally with the United States—as well as to the outskirts of Baghdad, which insurgents sought to control in order to launch attacks into the city.

Petraeus and Odierno agreed that the essence of the struggle in Iraq was (and remains) a competition between communities for power and resources. By filling the power vacuum, the U.S. military sought to buy the time and space for the Iraqi government to move forward with national reconciliation and improve its delivery of public services. U.S. troops showed that they were willing to emerge from their bases and place the defense of the Iraqi people above all else, which sent a clear message to the Iraqi public that U.S. forces would not be defeated. Many Iraqis stopped providing passive sanctuary to armed groups and, assured that the United States would protect them from reprisal, offered intelligence that enabled U.S. troops to target insurgents more accurately. Meanwhile, the United States reached out to previously hostile tribal and factional leaders, coaxing them to turn against al Qaeda and participate in the political process.

The surge accompanied and fostered other crucial internal changes. It coincided with and benefited from tectonic shifts within the Sunni community, as the Sunni nationalist insurgency and al

Qaeda began competing for dominance. Al Qaeda's efforts to impose a puritanical form of Islam angered the Sunni population, and the Sunni tribes, in a time-honored fashion, retaliated when their members were killed. At the same time, the Sunnis realized that they were losing ground to the Shiite militias and came to see Iran as a greater threat than the United States. These factors drove the Sunni tribes in Anbar to turn to the United States for support in a phenomenon known as the Sunni Awakening, which spread in similar ways to other parts of the country. When the Iraqi Shiites observed that the Sunnis were battling al Qaeda themselves and preventing insurgent attacks on the Shiite community, they became less tolerant of the Shiite death squads and militias, whose legitimacy rested on their defense of Shiites against Sunni aggression. This shift reached its climax in March 2008, when Iraqi Prime Minister Nouri al-Maliki felt that his government was being so undermined by the behavior of Jaish al-Mahdi, the Shiite militia led by the Iraqi cleric Muqtada al-Sadr, that he ordered military operations against it in Basra and Baghdad. The U.S.-supported operations decimated Jaish al-Mahdi, enhancing Maliki's standing and earning him the respect of Iraq's Sunnis as well. In short, the surge succeeded in changing Iraq's political environment, encouraging the Shiites and the Sunnis to bring the civil war to an end. The improvement in the security situation convinced partisans on both sides that they could achieve their political goals only by joining the political process.

SECURING THE SURGE

The unexpected drop in violence convinced many Americans that the war in Iraq had been won. The surge had undoubtedly met its stated aim of buying the time and space necessary for the Iraqi government to advance national reconciliation and, at least in theory, develop the capacity to provide adequate public services. Yet Iraq's parties did not take advantage of the opportunity to turn progress at the local level into national reconciliation. When Odierno replaced Petraeus in September 2008, the greatest threat to

Iraq's stability had become the legitimacy and capability of the government, rather than insurgents. Research and opinion polls showed that as the violence dropped, jobs and public services replaced security as the number one concern, and the government was not able to meet the public's growing expectations. I advised Odierno that we needed to meet these new hopes by preserving the fragile security gains and, at the same time, ensuring that our actions did not infringe on Iraqi sovereignty.

To quicken the pace of national reconciliation, Odierno attempted to integrate the ISF, which until that time had been predominately Shiite. From my close relationship with Maliki's advisers, I understood that the government remained suspicious of the Sunni Awakening and feared that by supporting it, the United States was creating a Sunni army that would overthrow the country's Shiite leadership. We sought to allay these concerns by pressuring the Iraqi government to place Sunni Awakening soldiers on its payroll, legitimizing them as local police forces and improving the ISF's sectarian balance. U.S. troops closely trained and monitored ISF troops, reporting instances of misconduct to the Iraqi government. As the ISF became more diverse and professional, the country became more secure.

Yet the annual United Nations Security Council resolution authorizing the presence of U.S. forces in Iraq was set to expire in December 2008, raising the possibility that the United States would have to depart the country immediately or remain there illegally, both of which would have threatened the gains made by the surge. To prevent either scenario, the U.S. and Iraqi governments entered negotiations over the U.S.-Iraq Status of Forces Agreement (SOFA), which would define the future of U.S. engagement in the country.

Iraqi officials bargained tenaciously during the SOFA negotiations and extracted significant concessions from the United States. They insisted on and won greater control over the actions of U.S. forces and secured a promise of their departure from population centers by the end of June 2009 and their total withdrawal by the end of 2011. The Bush administration even allowed Iraq the "primary right to exercise jurisdiction" over U.S. military members who committed "grave premeditated felonies," such as rape, and agreed that all suspects arrested by U.S. troops would be detained under warrant and held in Iraqi facilities. To the Iraqis, this meant that U.S. forces would be operating under the rule of law rather than the rule of war, as they had been since 2003.

The U.S. military reacted apprehensively to these demands, uncomfortable with the idea of U.S. soldiers falling under foreign legal authority and worried that the announcement of concrete dates for the troop withdrawals would boost insurgent morale. Some Iraqis expressed discomfort with the deal, too. For some of them, the idea of a security agreement permitting continued foreign occupation recalled the bitter memory of a century of colonial intervention in the country's affairs. The political elites, for their part, feared that Maliki was becoming increasingly authoritarian and was consolidating his power through higher oil revenues and the ISF's growing capacity. They suspected that the SOFA would bring U.S. forces under Maliki's control, preventing the United States from playing a brokering role or guarding against sectarian and undemocratic behavior.

As expected, politicians allied with Sadr voted against the agreement in the Iraqi parliament. Some Sunni leaders also opposed the SOFA, afraid that a U.S. pullout would increase Iran's influence over Iraq and expose the Sunni community to further attacks from Shiite elements in the ISF. Despite doubts among both the U.S. military and Iraqi factions, Iraq's parliament reached a consensus to sign the agreement once its various parties felt they had achieved three important conditions: passing a resolution that demanded political reform, securing a commitment to hold a national referendum on the SOFA in July 2009, and receiving letters of assurance from the United States that repeated Washington's commitment to protect the democratic process. Meanwhile, Maliki boosted his reputation by taking a hard line in the negotiations, establishing U.S. forces as guests of the Iraqi government rather than occupiers under a UN resolution.

The SOFA was signed along with a strategic framework agreement, which provided a possible glimpse of the future of U.S.-Iraqi ties. It affirmed "the genuine desire of [Iraq and the United States] to establish a long-term relationship of cooperation and friendship" across a range of areas, including culture, health, trade, energy, communications, security, and diplomacy. Together with the SOFA, the Strategic Framework Agreement solidified the coming shift in the United States' relationship with Iraq, from one of patronship to one of partnership.

EMBRACING IRAQI SOVEREIGNTY

On taking office, President Barack Obama followed his campaign pledge to end the Iraq war while honoring the SOFA signed with Iraq's government under the Bush administration. He engaged in an extensive policy review with Odierno, taking into consideration the opinions of those who thought that only a small residual force was necessary in Iraq as well as the ideas of those who argued that a defined pullout date would simply encourage the insurgents to lie low until U.S. forces departed. Obama chose the middle ground, ordering the end of combat operations and the reduction of U.S. troops to 50,000 by August 2010. The decision gave Odierno the flexibility he desired, within set deadlines, to determine the pace of the troop withdrawal so that he could respond to any military or political contingencies, such as parliamentary delays in holding elections or forming a goverment. Odierno implemented Obama's plan by shifting the mission of the remaining U.S. forces from counterinsurgency to stability operations, focusing on bolstering the ISF's capacity to protect the Iraqi people on their own.

The U.S. military required significant physical and strategic restructuring to accomplish this transformation. As we discussed how to make those necessary adjustments, Odierno and I began with the premise that the struggle in Iraq was essentially political. We agreed that the U.S. military could assist by training the ISF and preventing conflict but that only the Iraqis themselves could solve the underlying issues plaguing their country: tensions between Arabs and Kurds, Shiites and Sunnis, and local provinces and the national government. Although security in Iraq had greatly improved, the country had merely gone from being a failed state to being a fragile state, still beset with poor public services and subject to the pervasive influence of armed groups and foreign powers. As a result, Odierno instructed his commanders that the troop drawdown should not become the overriding focus of their mission. The United States had to help the Iraqi government develop the necessary state institutions to function properly on its own. Brigades were reorganized to further that goal, enabling U.S. State Department- led transition teams to build administrative capacity in provincial and local governments throughout Iraq.

Odierno provided his subordinates with the flexibility to determine when conditions in their respective areas were ripe for the shift. U.S. troops had to embrace Iraqi assertions of sovereignty as a sign of progress, even when they sometimes conflicted with U.S. advice. They also had to accept that the ISF were never going to be as proficient as U.S. troops. Odierno explained that the United States sought a strategic partnership with Iraq and that the way in which U.S. forces left the country would influence the long-term relationship between the U.S. and the Iraqi governments.

Odierno traveled the country to obtain on-the-ground progress reports from his commanders, considering it a success when they showed an in-depth understanding of what could cause instability in their areas and when they reported on how they were working closely with their U.S. civilian colleagues to address those issues through reconstruction project funds and technical assistance. Odierno encouraged his commanders to describe progress being made by the ISF in terms of the forces' relations with the local population, the operations they conducted, the circumstances in which they had requested U.S. assistance, and what further training they required.

As I prepared to depart Iraq in August 2010, it was clear that the close partnership between the U.S. military and the ISF had paid dividends. Accompanying Odierno as he toured the country to review the progress, I witnessed U.S. and ISF soldiers celebrating each time the United States transferred one of its bases to Iraqi forces, conducting ceremonies in which U.S. commanders symbolically delivered the keys to their Iraqi counterparts. The strong individual and institutional relationships between the two forces contributed to a growing sense of security across the country.

CHANGING ROLES

U.S. forces surveyed their respective regions for disruptive elements that could undermine the calm. Communal struggles persisted between Arabs and Kurds and Shiites and Sunnis; state institutions remained weak, as the central government and the provinces negotiated power-sharing arrangements; foreign powers, especially Iran (as well as Syria and Turkey), continued to meddle in Iraqi politics; and extremist groups, such as the remnants of al Qaeda and lingering Shiite militias, continued to foment trouble. Odierno understood that the very presence of U.S. troops could fuel instability, as groups would attack them in an attempt to gain credit for the impending U.S. withdrawal.

By viewing post-surge Iraq through this prism, the U.S. military focused its actions to provide the necessary resources and advice to those Iraqis attempting to smooth the points of friction. In September 2008, for instance, tensions arose between Arabs and Kurds in the northern Iraqi region of Diyala, and followed several months later in Kirkuk and Ninewa. The two sides came close to armed conflict over control of disputed territories in northern Iraq, which the Kurdistan Regional Government was seeking to incorporate within its federal region. The ISF and the Kurdish Pesh Merga (security forces) viewed each other with increasing suspicion and focused their energies on each other, allowing al Qaeda to exploit the situation by attacking various religious minority groups, including Christians, Shabaks, and Yezidis. Only mediation by U.S. officers prevented fighting from breaking out between the ISF and the Pesh Merga. At the request of Maliki and Massoud Barzani, president of the Kurdistan Region, Odierno devised a system of cooperation among the ISF, the Pesh Merga, and U.S. troops in operational centers, at checkpoints, and during patrols. This helped establish relationships between the leaders of the various forces, building mutual trust and confidence and restoring stability to the disputed territories.

As the June 2009 deadline for U.S. soldiers to leave Iraqi cities approached, Odierno accompanied Iraq's minister of defense, Abdul-Kader al-Obeidi, and minister of the interior, Jawad al-Bolani, around the country to assess the security situation and the ISF's performance. It was clear that security was continuing to improve and that joint operations with U.S. forces were hastening the ISF's development. After some initial growing pains, communication and collaboration between the U.S. military and the ISF had allowed Iraqi soldiers to take the lead, with U.S. forces largely providing background support. Although conditions varied across the country—in Basra, the ISF had largely taken command, whereas in Ninewa, U.S. soldiers compensated for a lack of adequate Iraqi forces by continuing their combat operations against al Qaeda— nearly all U.S. units had undertaken the transition from counterinsurgency to stability operations by early 2010, months ahead of schedule.

The implementation of the SOFA proceeded far more smoothly than either Iraqi or U.S. leaders had anticipated. In order to be ready to address potential violations of the agreement, the U.S. and Iraqi governments had established a number of joint committees covering a spectrum of security issues, including military operations, detainee affairs, and airspace control. There were only a few initial complaints issued by Iraqis about suspected U.S. violations of the agreement. Despite the initial fears of the U.S. military leadership, no U.S. soldier was ever arrested by the ISF and no issues of jurisdiction arose regarding U.S. soldiers. Meanwhile, the United States adhered strictly to the withdrawal timeline established by the SOFA, showing the Iraqis that the United States had no intention of occupying their country indefinitely. The deadline forced the U.S. military to relinquish power and allowed the Iraqis to assume command more quickly than might otherwise have happened. The United States demonstrated that it would leave with dignity, in partnership with the Iraqi government rather than under fire from insurgents.

The development of strong individual and institutional relationships between U.S. and Iraqi troops will likely continue as the two countries work to establish a long-term relationship. The rights and wrongs of the Iraq war will be debated for years to come. What will not be disputed, however, is the way in which the U.S. military learned from its initial blunders, adapted, retrained and reeducated its soldiers, transitioned seamlessly from counterinsurgency to stability operations, and strengthened the capacity of Iraqi forces.

THE STRUGGLE CONTINUES

Despite the successful transition from the surge to sovereignty in Iraq, challenges remain on the horizon for internal Iraqi politics and the U.S.-Iraqi relationship. The fraught formation of a governing coalition following Iraq's March 2010 national elections revealed how fragile the country's political institutions remain. Although Iraq's 2009 provincial elections had brought the Sunnis into local government and promoted reconciliation, the 2010 contest saw friction once again. Maliki accused former elements of Saddam Hussein's Baath Party, along with Syria, of masterminding continued attacks in Iraq. Some Shiite politicians, supported by Iran, sought to weaken the nationalist, nonsectarian Iraqiya Party, led by Ayad Allawi, by attempting to disqualify its candidates as former Baath Party members.

The Iraqiya Party overcame these challenges and narrowly won the election, with 91 seats, gaining the votes of most Sunnis and of a sizable proportion of secular Shiites. Maliki's Dawa Party came in a close second, with 89 seats, and for the next nine months, the two factions left Iraq in political limbo, with each side seeking to secure a majority in parliament in order to form a coalition government. Ironically, both the United States and Iran supported Maliki's bid to remain prime minister; U.S. leaders sought to broker a power-sharing arrangement between the two parties to keep Sadr's followers out of the government and strengthen reconciliation, whereas Iran hoped for a Shiite-dominated coalition. Maliki and Allawi grudgingly came to terms this past December, with Maliki retaining his post as prime minister and Allawi becoming head of the newly created National Council for Higher Policies, the purview of which remains uncertain.

Although a government has been formed, Iraq's political factions sadly missed an opportunity to secure the public's belief in the democratic system. Instead of demonstrating a peaceful transition of power and unity, the process revealed the lingering mistrust within Iraqi society, particularly among the ruling elites, who appeared ready to elevate their personal interests above the national good. Meanwhile, Iraqis remain skeptical of the large and unwieldy coalition assembled by Maliki, which enjoys few points of agreement and will have difficulty grappling with politically sensitive issues, such as federalism, the sharing of oil revenues, and the demarcation of internal borders. True reconciliation among Iraq's ethnic and religious groups thus remains elusive, and what progress has been achieved so far could unravel.

Meanwhile, the Obama administration's rhetorical emphasis on the troop withdrawal—meant for a domestic audience—has largely overshadowed the quiet but burgeoning strategic partnership between Iraq and the United States. Washington needs to devote adequate attention and resources to furthering the Strategic Framework Agreement, which established the basis for possible long-term cooperation between the two countries. Iraqi politicians from all communities, save the Sadrists, have voiced concern that the United States is too focused on withdrawing from Iraq, placing stability before democracy and strengthening Maliki's ability to maintain control of the country through the ISF rather than through the consent of Iraq's politicians or public. They have also expressed concern about Iran's ambitions and aspirations in Iraq—an issue that will loom over the country for years to come.

Iraq still has a long way to go before it becomes a stable, sovereign, and self-reliant country. Continued engagement by the United States can help bring Iraq closer to the American vision of a nation that is at peace with itself, a participant in the global market of goods and ideas, and an ally against violent extremists. Under the terms of the Strategic Framework Agreement, the United States should continue to encourage reconciliation, help build professional civil service and nonsectarian institutions, promote the establishment of checks and balances between the country's parliament and its executive branch, and support the reintegration of displaced persons and refugees. U.S. assistance is also needed to bolster Iraq's civilian control over its security forces, invest in the country's police units, and remove the Iraqi army from the business of policing. Should Washington fail to provide such support, there is a risk that Iraq's different groups may revert to violence to achieve their goals and that the Iraqi government may become increasingly authoritarian rather than democratic—undermining the United States' enormous investment of blood and treasure.

This article is part of the Foreign Affairs Iraq Retrospective.

It's Hard to Say Goodbye to Iraq

Why the United States Should Withdraw this December

Micah Zenko

In November 2008, representatives of U.S. President George W. Bush and Iraqi Prime Minister Nouri al-Maliki signed a Status of Forces Agreement (SOFA), which established the operational and legal framework for U.S. soldiers and their civilian counterparts in Iraq. The key line in the agreement was contained in Article 24: "All the United States Forces shall withdraw from all Iraqi territory no later than December 31, 2011." In a major speech a few months later, newly inaugurated U.S. President Barack Obama affirmed that he intended to uphold the deadline.

But it is proving difficult for the U.S. military to say goodbye to Iraq, after what has now amounted to a 21-year engagement, including nearly 4,000 days of no-fly zones and 3,000 days of stability operations since the first Gulf War. U.S. defense officials have recently begun begging and bluffing to compel Iraq's government to ask the United States to stay. In April, Admiral Michael Mullen, chairman of the Joint Chiefs of Staff, gave Maliki an ultimatum: "Should the Iraqi government desire to discuss the potential for some U.S. troops to stay," he warned, "it needs to start soon—very

MICAH ZENKO is a fellow in the Center for Preventive Action at the Council on Foreign Relations, and author of *Between Threats and War: U.S. Discrete Military Operations in the Post-Cold War World.*

soon—should there be any chance of avoiding irrevocable logistics and operational decisions we must make in the coming weeks."

Yet Baghdad seems unable to make up its mind. Some political leaders privately lobby for U.S. troops to stay, but only in training and advising roles. Still, most Iraqis and many members the Iraqi parliament are weary of a continued American military presence, which is problematic since U.S. officials insist that an updated SOFA be approved by the parliament. Iraqi President Jalal Talabani had requested that Baghdad's fractious political blocs decide by last Saturday whether to ask for an extension of U.S. troop presence into next year. They were unable to reach a consensus and have postponed additional negotiations on the topic "until further notice."

Still, according to anonymous U.S. officials, the White House is prepared to keep 10,000 ground troops in Iraq after the end of this year. It apparently has two reasons. The first is to prevent Iran from supplying improvised explosive devices and rockets to Shia militants in Iraq who have used such weapons to kill U.S. troops. According to U.S. officials, nine of the 15 U.S. soldiers who were killed in Iraq in June died from such attacks. The second is that somehow the mere presence of 10,000 U.S. troops will mitigate Iran's long-term influence in Iraq, which has been a proxy battlefield between Washington and Tehran for decades.

There are a few problems with this logic. For starters, it does not make sense for the United States to keep soldiers in Iraq to prevent Iranians from providing Iraqi Shias with weapons to kill U.S. soldiers in Iraq. As the Pentagon noted in its "Measuring Security and Stability in Iraq" report last summer, "Iran will likely continue providing Shi'a proxy groups in Iraq with funding and lethal aid, calibrating support based on several factors, including Iran's assessment of U.S. Force posture during redeployment." In other words, Iran will continue its behavior as long as there are U.S. soldiers in Iraq to target, which suggests that the surest and fastest way to prevent further bloodshed is to withdraw the remaining U.S. soldiers on schedule.

Further, no matter what the United States does, Iran will continue to try to influence Iraq. Tehran has a strategic interest in its neighbor's political makeup and will use a combination of soft-power initiatives—including outreach to sympathetic political parties, such as Dawa, Maliki's Islamic party—and providing weapons to Shia extremist groups for targeting U.S. forces and gaining the upper hand in the region. Countering those attempts should not primarily be the job of a diminished and constrained U.S. military presence; diplomats are better suited for such a mission, and the transition to a U.S. civilian-led mission in Iraq is already under way. After 2011, the U.S. civilian presence in Iraq will remain massive. The State Department will eventually deploy some 17,000 personnel at 15 sites across the country, 5,100 of whom will be security contractors.

If the 46,000 U.S. troops in Iraq now (and the 166,000 U.S. troops deployed there during the 2007 surge) have not been able to shut down the Iranian weapons pipeline, there is no reason to believe that the 10,000 troops the Obama administration would have stay in the country could do so. And even if Iran's weapons continued to flow into Iraq after 2011, the U.S. military would have few appealing options for addressing the problem along the 900-mile Iran-Iraq border.

The United States could choose to target assets and operatives outside of Iraq that are connected with Iran's Revolutionary Guard. But that would not be wise, either. In 2008, U.S. special operations forces did something similar when they killed Abu Ghadiya, an al Qaeda commander, in Sukkariyah, a city near Syria's border with Iraq. The mission did nothing to convince the Syrian government to close its borders to al Qaeda, which U.S. officials claimed Syria had been directly supporting. Such a move against Iran would be perceived as an attack on the state, and any resulting retaliation would needlessly place Americans in Iraq in immediate danger.

If the Obama administration believes that leaving troops in Iraq would prevent the impression that Iran is "driving us out," as a senior U.S. defense official put it, it should reconsider. The United States should not indefinitely maintain 10,000 troops in Iraq for second-order psychological reasons, such as attempting to alter the thinking of Tehran's opaque political leadership structure.

Furthermore, U.S. strategy in Iraq should not be based on what Tehran might say about it.

Instead, the United States ought to base its Iraq strategy on a clear-eyed assessment of national interests, which would mean ending the U.S. military presence, reducing the operation's financial burden on U.S. taxpayers, and providing assistance to Iraq so that it can defend its borders. Sooner or later (and probably sooner) Iraq must be able to protect its own sovereign territory. Whether it succeeds is not a matter of resources; as U.S. Secretary of Defense Leon Panetta recently noted, the "damn country has a hell of a lot of resources." It is primarily a matter of Baghdad's political will, which was lacking when 166,000 U.S. troops were fighting the Sunni-led insurgency at a cost of some $12 billion a month in 2007, and remains lacking today.

In the meantime, the United States should continue to help build up Iraq's military capacity. As in other countries, this effort should be led by the State Department in Washington and the U.S. embassy's Office of Security Cooperation in Baghdad. Efforts should include training Iraqi Ministry of Interior police and border forces, educating Iraqi officers at U.S. war colleges and academies, conducting military-military exchanges, and sharing intelligence. The United States could also help by selling Iraq advanced conventional weaponry; Iraq is reportedly interested in buying 36 F-16 fighter jets from Lockheed Martin.

If the Obama administration does convince Maliki to ask U.S. troops to stay, it must explain what the operational constraints of a new SOFA would be, and provide a new timetable for withdrawal. Moreover, in a war that two-thirds of U.S. citizens oppose and that has left 4,474 U.S. soldiers dead, Obama should be pressed to provide a clear and compelling reason why leaving 10,000 troops in Iraq is in the United States' national interest and, more specifically, how it would plausibly mitigate Iranian influence. Despite his mastery of rhetoric and eloquence, chances are that he will not be able to, which is why the United States should implement the 2008 SOFA now and finally end its military presence in Iraq.

The Problem With Obama's Decision to Leave Iraq

How to Salvage the Relationship Between Washington and Baghdad

Meghan L. O'Sullivan

I n April 2008, Ryan Crocker, who was then the U.S. ambassador to Iraq, told Congress, "In the end, how we leave and what we leave behind will be more important than how we came." Given President Barack Obama's announcement last Friday that all U.S. troops will leave Iraq by the end of the year, it is more important than ever to answer Crocker's implicit question about what, exactly, Washington will be leaving in its wake.

There is reason to worry. Iraq faces multiple political, security, and diplomatic challenges, and it is unclear how well it can meet those threats. Eight years after the toppling of Saddam Hussein, the country remains a fragile and complicated place. When pressed, Iraq's new political class has been able to forge compromises over contentious issues such as the role of Islam in government and how to ratify a new constitution. The Iraqi people resisted the worst forms of Iran's predations when they backed

MEGHAN L. O'SULLIVAN is Jeane Kirkpatrick Professor of the Practice of International Affairs at the John F. Kennedy School at Harvard University and Adjunct Senior Fellow at the Council on Foreign Relations. From 2004 to 2007, she was Deputy National Security Advisor for Iraq and Afghanistan.

Iraqi Prime Minister Nouri al-Maliki's crackdown on Iranian-affiliated militias in 2008.

But the foundations of the Iraqi state remain shallow. Divisions within Iraq's ruling elite run deep. A continued U.S. military presence would not have guaranteed peace and prosperity, but its removal increases the risks of failure in Iraq by eliminating the psychological backstop to a still delicate political system and by kicking open the door more widely to foreign interference.

The ostensible reason for America's withdrawal is that the two sides could not agree on the legal terms for an ongoing U.S. military presence—specifically, whether American troops would be subject to local laws. Indeed, Obama was right to make immunity for U.S. troops a deal-breaker. Yet this impasse was probably surmountable. After all, the issue arose during the negotiations that led to the successful completion of the 2008 security agreement between Washington and Baghdad. In that case, the two sides worked privately on an agreement that ultimately entailed some strategic ambiguity. Iraqis were able to claim that there were certain scenarios under which American soldiers would be held to Iraqi law; Americans could plausibly claim that such scenarios would never materialize.

Of course, 2008 is not 2011. And there is no question that the Iraqis bear much of blame for this outcome. But at a minimum, a successful outcome this time around would have required painstaking efforts by the United States to shape the political environment so that Iraqi leaders could say in public what many were saying in private: that their preference was for some number of American soldiers to stay.

Conditioning the scene would have taken an enormous amount of political commitment and capital. It would have required Washington's vigorous engagement—and possible deal-cutting—with powerful Iraqi actors across the political scene to approve a continued U.S. military presence, however limited. The team at the U.S. Embassy in Baghdad, which worked tirelessly on this negotiation, would not have been able to produce this outcome without extensive support from Washington, particularly the time and voice of the president and vice president. Neither had traveled to Baghdad for months; Obama apparently did not meet with the Iraqi delegation during the UN General Assembly in September.

Brokering a deal to keep U.S. troops in Iraq would also have necessitated more discipline from Washington. Once the U.S. side leaked the White House's intention to leave only 3,000 troops behind, the Iraqis were left with little incentive to take a major political risk to secure something so meager. Finally, getting a deal would also have required more flexibility from Washington, which insisted that immunity for U.S. forces be approved by Iraq's parliament. (The United States does not usually make it a practice to tell a country what it needs to do to make its own laws or international agreements binding.) All of these components of a successful negotiation were in short supply; collectively, they led to strategic failure.

Washington also leaves behind less than optimal prospects for a robust U.S.-Iraqi partnership. Five or ten years from now, the relationship will be more anemic, in part because groups opposed to American influence have now gained an upper hand and are likely to be strengthened in the interim. Note the recent statement from the Iranian- allied Iraqi lawmaker Muqtada al-Sadr. Apparently dissatisfied with the imminent departure of U.S. military personnel, Sadr declared all U.S. Embassy employees "occupiers" who should be "resisted." In addition, the nonmilitary bilateral relationship will be difficult to build without any forces on the ground. Last Friday's announcement complicated ambitions to expand the civilian footprint in Iraq—the U.S. State Department is putting plans to build consulates on hold due to security and cost concerns.

The United States also leaves behind a region where Iran's influence is growing. Tehran is on the offensive, as it has shown by announcing new nuclear enrichment plans, backing more aggressive attacks on U.S. troops in Iraq, and allegedly plotting to kill Saudi Arabia's ambassador in Washington. What, if any, plan the White House has for countering such belligerence is unclear. But it is inconceivable that any sensible strategy for addressing Iran would involve withdrawing all U.S. troops from Iraq.

Finally, the optics of how the United States leaves Iraq matter. The events of the last few days have given a negative gloss to nearly a decade of U.S. military involvement there. The focus has been almost exclusively on the breakdown in negotiations and the president's campaign promise to end the war in Iraq. Obama began his troop- withdrawal announcement with, "In my campaign, I promised . . ." An e-mail from the president to millions of Americans noted that the troops were coming home, that the costs of the war had been tremendous, and that, of course, he had delivered on a signature campaign pledge. There has been virtually nothing said about what has been achieved, what Americans and Iraqis can be proud of, or how the two countries will work together on a common agenda going forward.

Imagine a different scenario, one in which Obama and al-Maliki stood together and issued a joint statement on the decision to wind down the U.S. troop presence while pledging to remain steadfast partners. Such a rollout would have done better justice to the more than one million Americans who served in Iraq. It would have had a strategic importance as well. One of the core lessons learned from a decade of involvement in Iraq and Afghanistan is that you can win on the battlefield, but unless you control the narrative of what happened, you will not be successful.

While there is much to lament about the long U.S. involvement in Iraq, there is also a great deal to be proud of. Americans and Iraqis have shown enormous resilience and fortitude. Iraq has built new institutions and begun to fashion a path toward sustainable, representative government. And the region has opportunities today it never would have enjoyed under Saddam. If the U.S. government had to withdraw all troops from Iraq, its words should have put these developments in the context they deserve.

All, however, is not necessarily lost. While regrettable, last Friday's decision does not completely close the door on American interests in the region, or on the potential to improve the U.S.-Iraqi relationship. There will still be opportunities to promote common U.S.-Iraqi interests—the 2008 "strategic framework agreement" provides a template for a more robust, multidimensional partnership by declaring a commitment to educational exchanges, scientific cooperation, and diplomatic coordination.

Once emotions in both countries have calmed, Washington should intensify efforts to make the training mission that U.S. Secretary of Defense Leon Panetta is talking about a reality. The United States should also look at what sort of cooperation and support it can give to Iraq by air and sea without putting any U.S. military personnel on Iraqi soil. Congress should declare its intention to fund robust budget requests for the State Department and other U.S. agencies to make meaningful civilian cooperation possible.

Finally, Obama should consider making a visit to Iraq, where he can stand side by side with Maliki and put this chapter of American history into the right context—for Americans and for the region. One need not have agreed on the start of the war to finish it honorably.

The Iraq We Left Behind

Welcome to the World's Next Failed State

Ned Parker

Nine years after U.S. troops toppled Saddam Hussein and just a few months after the last U.S. soldier left Iraq, the country has become something close to a failed state. Prime Minister Nouri al-Maliki presides over a system rife with corruption and brutality, in which political leaders use security forces and militias to repress enemies and intimidate the general population. The law exists as a weapon to be wielded against rivals and to hide the misdeeds of allies. The dream of an Iraq governed by elected leaders answerable to the people is rapidly fading away.

The Iraqi state cannot provide basic services, including regular electricity in summer, clean water, and decent health care; meanwhile, unemployment among young men hovers close to 30 percent, making them easy recruits for criminal gangs and militant factions. Although the level of violence is down from the worst days of the civil war in 2006 and 2007, the current pace of bombings and shootings is more than enough to leave most Iraqis on edge and deeply uncertain about their futures. They have lost any hope that the bloodshed will go away and simply live with their

NED PARKER is Edward R. Murrow Press Fellow at the Council on Foreign Relations. He was a correspondent for the Los Angeles Times in Iraq in 2007-11.

dread. Acrimony in the political realm and the violence in the cities create a destabilizing feedback loop, whereby the bloodshed sows mistrust in the halls of power and politicians are inclined to settle scores with their proxies in the streets.

Both Maliki and his rivals are responsible for the slow slide toward chaos, prisoners of their own history under Saddam. Iraq today is divided between once-persecuted Shiite religious parties, such as Maliki's Dawa Party, still hungry for revenge, and secular and Sunni parties that long for a less bloody version of Saddam's Baath Party, with its nationalist ideology and intolerance of religious and ethnic politics. Meanwhile, the Kurds maneuver gingerly around the divisions in Baghdad. Their priority is to preserve their near autonomy in northern Iraq and ward off the resurrection of a powerful central government that could one day besiege their cities and bombard their villages, as Baghdad did throughout the twentieth century.

All sides hold the others responsible for all the friends and family killed during the Saddam era and the civil war that followed the U.S. invasion. All of Iraq's political leaders seem to live by the maxim that no enemy can become a partner, just a temporary ally; betrayal lurks around every corner. Each politician grabs as much power as he can, and unchecked ambition, ego, and historical grudges lead them all to ignore the consequences of their behavior for Iraq's new institutions and its society.

Maliki's tactics closely echo the pattern laid down by his predecessors, from Iraq's post- Ottoman monarchs to its first prime minister, Abdul Karim Kassem, to Saddam himself: put yourself first, and guard power with a ruthless security apparatus. Maliki's opponents, including his secular rival Ayad Allawi, the head of the Iraqiya Party, have given no indication they would act any differently. In the last year, Maliki has chipped away at safeguards for democracy, stocking the country's Human Rights Ministry with loyalists and using the state's anticorruption offices to target political enemies. Maliki's harassment and persecution of anyone deemed a threat to himself or his party has dramatically reduced freedom throughout Iraq. Most ominously for his country, and himself, Maliki, through his bullying and nepotistic rule, threatens to cause his own undoing and push Iraq back into civil war.

ABSENTEE WASHINGTON

This was not the Iraq the United States envisioned as it planned its invasion less than a decade ago. After toppling Saddam in 2003, U.S. policy aimed to create a democratic state that enshrined civil liberties; national reconciliation; a fair, apolitical judiciary; and freedom of speech. However, this goal was jeopardized from day one of the U.S. occupation by a series of debilitating blunders: not sending enough U.S. forces to secure the country, dissolving the old Iraqi military, and allowing a draconian purge of Baath Party members from civilian ministries. It was only belatedly, in Iraq's darkest hour, that the Bush administration sent thousands more troops to stop the civil war that had erupted. During the "surge," in 2007, the United States forced the ruling Shiite religious parties to take steps toward making peace with the Sunnis, blocked blatantly political arrests, and worked to marginalize, if not jail, officials implicated in violence. The hope was that improved security would allow Iraq to reach stability and acquire the trappings of liberal governance.

Maliki and his colleagues are not the only ones to blame for the dashing of these hopes and the slide away from democracy. Since the last months of the Bush administration and the beginning of the Obama presidency, rather than concentrate on shoring up democratic principles, as it had during the surge, Washington has instead focused on securing its long-term strategic relationship with Baghdad, especially with the prime minister, so that it could more easily withdraw U.S. forces. In the process, the United States failed to capitalize on the gains of the U.S. troop surge—the Iraqi people's renunciation of religious extremists and desire for normalcy—thereby damaging the chances that a unified, nonsectarian government could emerge.

Washington's biggest mistake of recent years came in the summer of 2010, when the United States dropped the pretense of neutrality by backing Maliki for the post of prime minister over Allawi—even though Allawi's party list had received more votes in the national elections held in March. U.S. officials argued that only a Shiite Islamist had the credibility and legitimacy to serve as prime minister and disparaged any alternative to Maliki. But by anointing Maliki, a devout Shiite who already had Iran's endorsement, the United States gave him the confidence to avoid serious compromises with Allawi, a secular Shiite supported by the country's Sunnis.

In November 2010, Maliki and Allawi reached a power-sharing agreement, sponsored by the Kurdish government in Erbil and Washington, in which Maliki was supposed to relinquish his direct command of the security forces and his tight grip on the cabinet and most ministries. The agreement awarded the Defense Ministry to Iraqiya and appointed Allawi to head a new consultative policy body. U.S. officials bragged that they had outmaneuvered Iran and midwifed a nonsectarian government in Baghdad.

But Washington quickly disengaged from actually ensuring that the provisions of the deal were implemented. U.S. Vice President Joseph Biden, the Obama administration's leading figure on Iraq policy, was largely absent from Iraq for nearly a year as the power-sharing arrangement unraveled. At the U.S. embassy in Baghdad, officials complained in private about Maliki's refusal to share power as he had promised, but they kept quiet in public, even as Maliki's military command stepped up its campaign of harassment and arrests of those considered rivals. When I was in Baghdad last June, I asked a U.S. diplomat why the embassy had said nothing about an ongoing crackdown against pro-democracy activists, including an incident in which Iraqi security agents had beaten protesters in broad daylight. He said that although U.S. officials had a "regular" dialogue with Maliki about human rights, Washington's "overriding focus and concern" was building a security relationship with the Iraqi government. But by turning a blind eye to Maliki's encroaching authoritarianism, U.S. officials allowed Iraq's political culture to disintegrate. (It was this disarray that also made it impossible for U.S. officials to get Iraq's leaders to push an immunity agreement through parliament so that a small number of U.S. troops could stay on after 2011.) Rather than help Iraq move forward, the United States allowed the country to drift back toward sectarianism and authoritarian rule.

The political situation in Baghdad hit a new low last December. The day after the last U.S. soldier left the country, Maliki suddenly called for the arrest of Iraq's Sunni vice president, Tariq al-Hashimi, on charges of running death squads. With this move, Maliki abandoned any lingering pretense that he was interested in national reconciliation and undermined the promises that he and U.S. President Barack Obama had made just days before in Washington, when they declared Iraq a stable democracy. Hashimi fled to Kurdistan, and the country's political process was plunged into limbo. The crisis exposed the artificial, Potemkin-village-like nature of Iraq's democratic system and how swiftly the feuds among Iraq's national leaders could endanger the state.

No political figure, no matter how high ranking, now doubts Maliki's ability to harness the law and the state to his ambitions. Still, Maliki lacks the authority to eliminate all his enemies, by virtue of being enmeshed in a parliament-based system, which was imposed by the United States after 2003. But he will keep striving for absolute power, using fear, intimidation, and cronyism. The opposition will conspire against him and attempt to sabotage his policies, positive or negative, out of the desire to see him fail. But handicapped by their own divisions, they will never succeed in ousting him. This corrosive deadlock will only fan further disillusionment with the current order, sending the political system hurtling toward implosion. One of three outcomes—all dangerous—will likely result.

First, some specific event or series of events—for example, the local and national elections expected in 2013 and 2014, respectively, or an escalation of the campaign of arrests against Maliki's foes—could trigger violence involving Iraq's tribes, sects, ethnicities, and parties. Second, the ineffectual rule of the central government could lead Sunni and Shiite regional leaders to carve out their own autonomous zones, leaving Iraq a state in name only, a prospect that could also ignite bloodshed if Baghdad refuses to recognize those boundaries or the provinces begin to fight over territory. Third, Shiite political figures and military officers could mount a coup, claiming the current government was endangering the country and declaring special rule for an emergency period. Repressive crackdowns would follow, triggering a cycle of retributive violence.

To save Iraq from these fates—any one of which would prove disastrous and would mark a total defeat for the United States in terms of its aims for the country—Washington must push Baghdad to honor the power-sharing agreements reached over a year ago and take concrete steps toward transparent governance, the rule of law, and national reconciliation. As much as Maliki will try to resist U.S. efforts to rein him in, he still believes that the United States can help him rebuild Iraq. He is caught between his grand ambition to attain affluence for his country, making Iraq an envy of nations, and his roots as an underground Islamic revolutionary. If he sees his abandonment by Washington as spelling the end to his rule or leading Iraq down the path of international isolation, as Saddam once led the country, he will be susceptible to pressure.

THE AFTERLIFE OF THE EMERALD CITY

To fully understand just how Iraq's current rulers work, it helps to visit the government in the Green Zone, 3.9 square miles of fortified territory in the heart of Baghdad. In the Saddam era, the neighborhood was called Karradat Mariam, after a local woman who cared for the poor. The district's homes, palaces, hotels, and monuments stood as garish displays of the Baath regime's wealth and pretensions. After the U.S. invasion in 2003, the U.S. military took control of the area and formalized its boundaries with blast walls and barbed wire. Then, in January 2009, when the United States ceded control over Iraqi security, Maliki became the lord of the Green Zone. Much like his U.S. predecessors, he spoke of opening the major highway that cuts through the restricted area to ease people's daily lives. But also like his U.S. predecessors, he was unable to keep his promise: the world outside proved too dangerous. Instead, Maliki's rule of the Green Zone became all-encompassing. Only those with the proper badges or escorted by someone with a government-issued Green Zone identification card can enter. (Those badges have become a source of corruption: according to U.S. military officers and Iraqis living around the area, one can be had for $10,000.) The beggars, widows, and families with sick relatives who once made a pilgrimage to the gates of the parliament building in the Green Zone to beg lawmakers for help are now barred from entry.

Maliki has mimicked many of the hierarchical controls created during the U.S. occupation. His office splits Green Zone badges into the same color-coded ranks (blue for the highest level of access, orange and red for the lowest) as did the United States, and Maliki awards badges to buy influence and patronage, just as U.S. officials once did. During the years of U.S. control, the U.S. Army stationed military police and army units to police and defend the Green Zone. Maliki has his own version: in late 2008, he created the Baghdad Brigade, a special unit that guards the area's gates and patrols its private roads. The brigade, which operates outside the normal chain of command, is comprised of soldiers from the country's Shiite heartland sympathetic to Maliki and his Dawa Party. (The religious nature of the force is visible on holidays, when banners depicting Shiite icons hang from the Green Zone's entrances.)

Moreover, Maliki has made the management of his office a family affair, to the point where some high-ranking government officials now wonder, as they told me, whether they serve a family or a state. This has created an irony obvious to many Iraqis: at a time when the rest of the Arab world is rejecting family rule, Maliki has surrounded himself with his kin and others from his birthplace of Twaireej, a rural area south of Baghdad. His son Ahmed, who is deputy to the chief of staff and in charge of his father's personal security, is arguably the most powerful person in Maliki's office.

He has gained particular notoriety for his consolidation of property in the Green Zone, which he has achieved by ordering the Baghdad Brigade to seize houses belonging to Iraqis and foreign contractors. These seizures have driven most Western companies out of the Green Zone. The Iraqi government does have legitimate reasons for wanting to ease out those Western firms that claimed land in the Green Zone after 2003. But such heavy-handed tactics—and the fact that the seized property has largely remained under Ahmed's control—have created the impression that Maliki's inner circle is mostly interested in enriching itself.

Maliki has also deployed his forces to intimidate and hamper his enemies. After the announcement of the arrest warrant against Hashimi in December, for example, Maliki deployed tanks outside the homes of Hashimi and other Iraqiya leaders; forces from the Baghdad Brigade required guests to present their credentials before going inside. He has dangled security as a carrot, awarding bodyguard battalions to allies while refusing to grant a similar request to a senior elected Sunni official whom he dislikes, despite the danger to his rival's life.

PALACES AND PRISONS

The greatest symbol of Maliki's strength in the Green Zone is a compound known as Camp Honor, the site of a bombed-out palatial meeting hall, built by Saddam in the 1990s, whose ceiling has a mural of Iraqi soldiers fighting U.S. troops. The U.S. military turned it into a base, and then, in 2006, it became the headquarters for an Iraqi army division. Today, the unkempt grounds are home to the giant palace, overgrown weeds, prefabricated houses, and shipping containers.

Since 2009, Camp Honor has also been the site of the private detention center overseen by Maliki's military office, which supervises all security operations and whose authority supersedes that of the Interior and Defense Ministries. In an infamous case from October 2009, Iraqi counterterrorism and regular army units grabbed more than 430 Sunni men in Mosul on the orders of that office.

The prisoners were first held in Camp Honor and then transferred to a secret prison at Baghdad's Muthanna Air Base, where they were discovered in March 2010 by officials from the Human Rights Ministry. Looking to avoid a controversy so shortly after the national elections held earlier that month, Maliki agreed to shut down the Muthanna jail. But he refused to relinquish control of the Camp Honor detention facility despite having pledged to do so. A year later, a committee of Iraqi lawmakers toured the jail and threatened to expose its findings publicly; in response, the government announced Camp Honor's formal closure. Yet as Iraqi parliamentarians and other government officials told me, Camp Honor in fact remains open as a secret jail for prisoners captured by Maliki's elite forces.

There are alarming signs that those held there continue to be tortured to extract confessions; then, once the desired testimony is obtained, they are sent off to regular, legally recognized prisons. Last May, the International Committee of the Red Cross wrote a confidential letter to Maliki demanding full access to the jail. (I obtained a copy through my work as a reporter for the *Los Angeles Times*.) Based on interviews with former detainees at Camp Honor, the Red Cross claimed that it had uncovered evidence of systematic torture and gross mistreatment, including rape and electric shock to the genitals. It wrote that it had learned that Iraqi judges had been present during some of the torture sessions to extract confessions. The Red Cross also added that it knew of three other secret Green Zone jails connected to Camp Honor that remained active and hid detainees in case of any international or local inspections. When I asked about the letter, the Red Cross declined to comment.

Last December, I met a middle-aged Iraqi man, Abu Ibrahim (this was an assumed name; he feared for retribution from military units close to Maliki), who told me that he had been picked up by Iraqi counterterrorism soldiers in a raid on his Baghdad neighborhood a few months earlier. Soldiers burst into his house in the middle of the night. A masked informant identified him and his father as suspected terrorists. He said he was first taken to the main airport in Baghdad, where he was well treated, thanks to the presence of U.S. forces. But once the counterterrorism troops drove him to the Green Zone, the treatment became rougher. For three days, he was brought to a cluster of trailers for interrogation, where he said he was chained to a bar and left to dangle until he passed out. The guards yelled, "Are you al Qaeda? Are you Baathist?" They later took him into a nearby trailer where a judge attached to the counterterrorism force was reviewing his file. The judge expressed doubts about the secret informant who had accused him of terrorism and ordered his release.

Another judge, however, refused to free his father, who had been a high-ranking officer in the Saddam-era army. Weeks after Abu Ibrahim was released, an intermediary told him that the secret informant would be willing to drop the allegations against his father in exchange for money. U.S. military officers and Iraqi human rights inspectors have uncovered a familiar pattern for those held in Iraqi jails: a security officer or an informant demands money for a detainee to be released, leading to protracted negotiations. But in the case of Abu Ibrahim's father, before any talks could take shape, the middleman disappeared. Now, Abu Ibrahim does not know if someone will ask him for money again or what will become of his father.

The situation is unlikely to improve anytime soon, as any investigator from the Human Rights Ministry or any official from any other government office who is brave enough to try to probe the jails would face immediate persecution. Three investigators have already fled the country, and those remaining are terrified. One former Iraqi official who worked on human rights issues and left the country last year because he was afraid for his safety told me that Maliki and the Dawa Party were essentially free to carry out whatever they liked in their jails. "Everything is under their control," he said. "It's easy for them to accuse anyone and destroy him."

EASY MONEY

Endemic corruption within the army and the police not only contributes to such prisoner abuse but also feeds into broader, more systemic problems within Iraq's security apparatus. The culture of graft leads to crippling inefficiencies and dangerous gaps: commanders pad military payrolls with soldiers who do not exist, military officers and ministry officials receive kickbacks on contracts for everything from food supplies to defense equipment, and senior officials create skeleton companies to pilfer money from the Treasury.

The toxic brew of corruption undermines any hopes for reform and improved governance. Adel Abdul Mahdi, who was Iraq's vice president until he resigned last summer in protest over Maliki's bloated cabinet and the culture of entitlement among officials, told me that corruption is so pervasive that it is blocking the provision of basic services. For example, as he explained, "mafias" in business and the government make money off the lack of progress in the electricity sector through overpriced contracts and sales funneled to politically connected but inefficient firms.

No political party or faction is immune to the lure of easy money, fed by the state's lucrative oil revenues and the lax controls on how cash is spent. The loyalty of a lawmaker, cleric, commander, or tribal leader can be bought with houses, cars, and cash. A longtime Iraqi civil servant close to Maliki's Dawa Party explained to me how it works: political figures set up shell companies, helmed by a trusted businessperson or relative, that then bid to deliver goods or services to the government. The contracts, whether for building a sewage line or beautifying the Baghdad highway, are consistently overpriced, allowing the companies to divert revenues and assets to the foreign bank accounts of government officials. An electricity official told me that the Electricity Ministry regularly purchases equipment for its distribution department that is purportedly German but is in fact cheap Chinese or Iranian knockoffs; similarly, a state-employed pharmacist in Baghdad complained about the cheap medicine that the government imports with no concern for quality because officials get kickbacks from particular companies or importers.

This culture of corruption filters up to the highest levels of government: even Iraq's national budget is shrouded in mystery, with appropriations announced and spent with little transparency. Baghdad has spent more than $400 billion since 2004, but the government is only now preparing to release a final account of its budgets from 2004 to

2009. Most of the cash spent will likely never be properly accounted for. In 2011, Baghdad reported that it did not know how much of the $25 billion that the central government had advanced to ministries, local governments, and state companies as of the middle of 2010 had actually been spent or if any excess funds could be returned.

Iraq's opaque finances create an atmosphere in which misdealings flourish. High-level politicians and officials can quickly put a halt to any investigation into wrongdoing among their associates or underlings. In April 2009, for example, Iraq's Commission on Public Integrity launched an investigation into Abdul Falah al-Sudani, then the trade minister and a member of a branch of Maliki's Dawa Party, for allegedly embezzling millions of dollars in public funds. A month after a shootout in central Baghdad between his staff and investigators, Sudani tried to flee the country and was briefly jailed. But almost a year later, a judge dismissed the case against him.

Those who have worked in the state's anticorruption bodies are bleak about the future. They have been blocked too many times by the powerful and realize that their lives are in danger. Some have been killed. The head of the Commission on Public Integrity resigned in September, frustrated by his inability to pursue corruption charges against high officials. Maliki replaced him with someone considered to be more pliant and less likely to antagonize those in power. In Baghdad, I met with an anticorruption official who showed me a number of veiled threats he had received on his cell phone from the boss of a company suspected of funneling money to the Dawa Party. One text message read, "Is it acceptable some government figures would provoke you to be against us? Do you think a big company like ours would not know about this?" It went on to say, "We are requesting that God protects you." The official was worried for his safety. He now never leaves home without a bodyguard. "Committing murder in Iraq is casual," he said, "like drinking a morning cup of coffee."

DASHED HOPES

Disenchantment with corruption and government dysfunction has spread to Basra, the oil-rich city in Iraq's Shiite south. It was here, with his 2008 campaign against the Shiite militias that were terrorizing ordinary Iraqis, where Maliki showed himself a bold leader willing to confront powerful Shiite armed groups even if it might cost him his job. Maliki's popularity soared; having saved the city from chaos, he was viewed as the best hope for security and development. But four years later, those hopes have largely been dashed: Basra is marked by open ponds brimming with sewage, sporadic electricity, and shantytowns made from looted sheet metal and bricks. Looking at the convoys of American and European oil workers driving across town and the two new luxury hotels that have opened in recent years, locals are sure that the money made from their oil fields is being whisked off to Baghdad.

Today, many local businesspeople and politicians believe that the creation of an autonomous region in the province of Basra is the only way to save it from poverty and the yoke of a corrupt elite in the capital. They are angry that Baghdad controls security and directs spending in the province, holding back funds from the local government in an effort to extend its dominance over the wealthy region. Last February, popular demonstrations in the province over poor services and official corruption forced the Dawa Party's choices for governor and chair of the provincial council to resign. (Protests have also forced the resignation of governors in two other Shiite provinces.) In late 2010, Basra's council voted in favor of a referendum on federalism, but the central government simply ignored the motion. Meanwhile, public anger in Basra and among

Shiite communities across the country prompted the Iraqi Shiites' most revered spiritual guide, Grand Ayatollah Ali al-Sistani, whose endorsement is readily sought by the Shiite political elite, to refuse all meetings with elected officials, including Maliki. Local politicians in Basra are sensitive to the popular mood, and even figures from Maliki's political slate feel they must assert their independence from Baghdad.

The new chair of the provincial council, Sabah al-Bazouni, who represents a branch of Maliki's Dawa Party, told me of Basra's woes: closed factories, electricity blackouts in the summer, miles of slums, dried-out irrigation canals. He wondered how the province that supplies 70 percent of the country's oil could be so poor. He said that Basra should be able to hold a referendum on greater autonomy, even over the objections of Maliki and the government in Baghdad.

If Basra does manage to become an autonomous region, Bazouni argues that the province should also gain the right to negotiate all future oil contracts in its territory, as well as manage its own port and borders and keep its own security forces. It would send back revenues to the Iraqi central government according to the national law, when it is finally passed, and whatever agreements Basra reached with Baghdad. The experiment could serve as a model for the capital's relationships with other restive regions, such as the two Sunni-led provinces currently also requesting independence. Of course, it could also cause splits, perhaps violent ones, within the country's Shiite majority. Those officials, such as Maliki, who advocate a strong national government could fall into conflict with their local counterparts who want greater power and control of Basra's lucrative resources. The temptation of being able to control a nearly autonomous region could also spark fighting among the local branches of Shiite parties, each of which sees itself as the rightful ruler of the wealthy region. Indeed, it was such competition that drove Basra to lawlessness before Maliki's intervention in 2008. Basra's residents seem to recognize these dangers, yet because they view Baghdad as pilfering their wealth, they see no better option.

"THE RIGHTEOUS HAVE THEIR OPPONENTS"

Faced with the prospect of his Shiite base splintering, Maliki has taken to fanning public fears of Iraq's Sunni minority. He seems to think that if he can keep Iraq's Shiites afraid of the Sunnis, they will not dare break with him and risk jeopardizing Shiite dominance of the political process. Maliki has accordingly begun to emphasize the Sunni atrocities committed during the Saddam era and the recent civil war. "Any successful person has enemies; the righteous have their opponents. Moses has his pharaoh, and every Hussein has his Yazid," Maliki said in a speech on New Year's Day, referring to the caliph who massacred Imam Hussein and his followers in the seventh century, giving birth to the modern-day schism between Shiites and Sunnis.

Such a strategy marks a break from Maliki's rhetoric in 2008, when, in order to extend his writ, he used the national army to fight Shiite militias and explored the idea of forming alliances with Sunni leaders. These relationships were abandoned in the raw politics of the 2010 national elections and the ensuing competition between Maliki and Allawi. In Maliki's subsequent bid to consolidate his power, he has come to rely more and more on fundamentalist Shiite parties. Since the elections, Maliki and his supporters have polarized the country's politics by trying to arrest Sunni politicians and announcing a series of foiled terrorist plots by Sunnis.

As a result, whereas two years ago many Sunnis viewed Maliki favorably, they now perceive him as an Iranian-backed despot out to destroy their community. According to former Sunni allies of Maliki, the Sunni community now fears that if Maliki hangs on to power, he will continue persecuting Sunnis with arbitrary arrests and intimidation campaigns. The Speaker of parliament, Osama al-Nujaifi, a Sunni from the Iraqiya bloc, has warned that if Baghdad continues to carry out such hostile actions, the Sunni population will be forced to declare their own autonomous regions. Indeed, many Sunni leaders now champion self-rule, an idea they opposed in 2005, when it was legally enshrined in the constitution (an article that Maliki continues to ignore). At the time, Sunni leaders viewed federalism as a recipe for Iraq's destruction and loathed the Kurds for their autonomy in the north. Today, they see the way the Kurds have thrived as proof that the only way to get a fair distribution of Iraq's wealth and to protect themselves from Baghdad is by embracing a federalist Iraq.

Last October, after security forces from Baghdad arrested dozens of aging former Baathists in the Sunni-majority Salahuddin Province, Salahuddin became the first Sunni region to call for a federal system. The recent history of Samarra, a strategically important city in Salahuddin and home to the sacred Askariya Mosque, provides a measure of the toll that Iraq's sectarian battles have taken on ordinary citizens. The city was once a model of the country's rich cross-cultural traditions, with its gold-domed mosque worshipped at by Shiites and tended by the city's majority Sunni population. But in 2006, al Qaeda in Iraq blew up the sanctuary, thereby igniting the country's civil war. The city's streets belonged to al Qaeda and its foot soldiers, who terrorized the local population. Now, six years later, the violence has subsided, and Shiite pilgrims are again traveling to pray in Samarra—but the shrine remains walled off with giant cement barriers that make it look like a maximum-security prison. Samarra's Sunni residents, who once prayed by the shrine and celebrated their weddings there, largely keep their distance. Men stand idle in front of empty clothing shops and hotels that once catered to pilgrims but are now effectively sealed off from commerce. Even locals have stopped shopping in the city's center so as to avoid the national police who harass those who come too close to the shrine.

The more Baghdad imposes its will on Sunni areas, the greater the chances for wider sectarian unrest. With no plan to break the country's political stalemate, the only course left for all sides is brinkmanship, with escalating Sunni demands for freedom and Baghdad answering back with intimidation. Even the Iraqi Kurds are encouraging the Sunnis to push for self-rule: they believe that if the Sunnis, traditionally hostile to Kurdish ambitions, embraced federalism, it would legitimize their own privileges and prevent Baghdad from ever trying to encroach on their authority.

Federalism could indeed end up being an effective mechanism for the country's Shiites, Sunnis, and Kurds to live together peacefully—but for it to work, a process of authentic national reconciliation would have to come first. Without shared decision-making in government, inclusive institutions, and trust and respect for the law, federalism would lead to the splintering of Iraq, turning the country into a proxy battlefield between Iran and the Sunni Muslim world. In this scenario, Iraq would exist only in name, leaving a collection of territories often at war with one another and at the mercy of foreign powers. Civilians would be subjected to terrorist attacks, caught in the middle of the ensuing regional struggles for oil and water. The notion of Iraq as a modern nation-state would fade, relegated to the ranks of failed twentieth-century colonial experiments.

SALVAGING THE AMERICAN LEGACY

The only hope Iraq has of escaping a future of war or corrupt, authoritarian rule is for the United States and the international community to start pushing hard for power sharing and democracy. Since Iraq's 2010 elections, Washington has completely failed on this score. But U.S. officials must not stay silent in the face of illegal detentions and crackdowns on civil liberties; neither should they back away from the power-sharing agreements they helped sponsor for the sake of short-term political considerations. Even with U.S. soldiers gone from the country, the United States retains leverage over Iraq. It can and should, for example, threaten to keep Iraq locked in its so-called Chapter 7 status in the United Nations, which deprives Iraq of full sovereignty and requires it to make reparations payments to Kuwait. And it should warn Iraq that it will cancel the sale of U.S. fighter jets, tanks, and surveillance equipment to the government unless it changes course. Iraq's leaders need to know that the international community has "redlines," and that secret prisons, the use of torture to extract confessions, and the harassment of democracy activists will not be tolerated. As for the danger of pushing Baghdad closer to Tehran, although Iran would gladly smother Iraq in a suffocating embrace, Iraq's own tortuous history of war with its neighbor means that Iraq will continue to seek a relationship with the West in part to counterbalance Tehran.

The local elections in 2013 and the national elections the year after will be a test of whether Iraq's leaders indeed believe in representative government or whether those in power now will try to hold on to it by any means necessary. Maliki is currently pursuing a number of officials on the electoral commission's staff with corruption investigations. And in January 2011, he won a court ruling that placed the commission under his authority, rather than under the parliament's. Whereas some Iraqi officials wonder if the next elections will be free and fair, several former U.S. military officers wonder if the elections will happen at all.

The United States must ensure that they do and that they are free and fair, and it must not countenance any democratic backsliding for the sake of political expediency. Confronting Maliki and his government on abuses and political arrests may strain relations, but ignoring such topics has only helped lead Iraq to its current, deeply troubled state. If Iraq slips into dictatorship or war, this will be the United States' legacy in the country. But Iraq should not be written off. With outside help, it could still manage to muddle through with an elected government that is somewhat accountable and somewhat representative. Such an outcome would go a long way toward redeeming the United States' disastrous misadventure there.

This article is part of the Foreign Affairs Iraq Retrospective.

Is Iraq on Track?

Democracy and Disorder in Baghdad

Antony J. Blinken, Norman Ricklefs, Ned Parker

MORNING IN MESOPOTAMIA

Antony J. Blinken

Ned Parker's article "The Iraq We Left Behind" (March/April 2012) gives the impression that Iraq is a hybrid of North Korea and Somalia, part ruthless dictatorship and part lawless wasteland: in short, "the world's next failed state." Leaving aside the inherent contradiction in describing a country as both authoritarian and anarchic, Iraq today bears little resemblance to the caricature portrayed in these pages.

The article glossed over, or ignored altogether, the clear, measurable progress Iraq has made in the few short years since it lurched to the brink of sectarian war. Since U.S. President Barack Obama took office with a commitment to end the war responsibly and initiated the drawdown of 144,000 troops, violence in Iraq has declined and remains at historic lows—a trend that has continued since the last U.S. troops departed late last year. Weekly security incidents fell from an average of 1,600 in 2007-8 to fewer than 100 today. Meanwhile, since 2005, oil production, the lifeblood of Iraq's

ANTONY J. BLINKEN is Deputy Assistant to the President of the United States and National Security Adviser to the Vice President.

NORMAN RICKLEFS is a consultant specializing in Iraqi security-sector reform and government relations. He has served as a Political Adviser to the Commanding General of Australian forces in Iraq and as a Senior Adviser to Iraq's Interior Minister.

economy, is up 50 percent, to almost three million barrels per day, providing the revenue that enabled lawmakers to pass a $100 billion budget in mid-February. Recent months have also seen unprecedented steps toward Iraq's reintegration with the region, including the appointment of a Saudi ambassador to Baghdad for the first time since 1990, visits to Iraq by senior Emirati and Jordanian officials, the settlement of Iraq's dispute with Kuwait over Saddam Hussein's confiscation of Kuwaiti aircraft, and Baghdad's playing host to the Arab League summit. U.S. military forces were critical to setting the conditions for these achievements. They succeeded, at great cost, in restoring a measure of stability when all seemed lost and in training an Iraqi army that is now defying doubters and capably providing security for the country. These advances created the time and the space for what U.S. Vice President Joseph Biden sees as the most important development in Iraq in recent years: politics supplanting violence as the dominant means for the country's various factions to settle their disputes and advance their interests.

For the past two years, critics repeatedly and mistakenly warned that a string of political crises, over the election law, the de-Baathification process, the election itself, and the formation of a government, would lead to renewed sectarian violence. Each time, however, the Iraqis resolved their differences through the political process, not violence, with quiet and continuous assistance from the United States.

Parker lauds as a golden age in Iraqi politics the period from late 2007 through late 2008, which he attributes to the large U.S. troop presence and the U.S. government's focus on promoting democracy. During that purported halcyon era, charges of terrorism leveled against a Sunni Arab politician led followers of the Shiite cleric Muqtada al- Sadr, the Sunni Arab parties, and those loyal to the secular Shiite leader Ayad Allawi to boycott the parliament for eight months, despite the presence of more than 150,000 U.S. troops in the country. A similar boycott early this year, when all U.S. troops were gone, lasted just two months.

STILL THE ONE

Parker also claims that the Obama administration turned its attention away from Iraq after the last Iraqi election, in March 2010, and abandoned the democratic principles for which the United States had fought. In fact, during the period he describes, the "largely absent" vice president made four visits to Iraq, spoke on the phone dozens of times with senior Iraqi officials from every major bloc, and, at Obama's request, chaired a monthly cabinet-level meeting on Iraq. I and other senior U.S. officials based in Washington, including Deputy National Security Adviser Denis McDonough and Deputy Secretary of State Thomas Nides, each made multiple trips to Iraq. Most important, the U.S. embassy in Baghdad, led by Ambassador James Jeffrey, was as engaged with Iraqi leaders, day in and day out, as at any point since the 2003 invasion. In virtually every meeting and public statement, we reaffirmed the United States' commitment to the rule of law and Iraq's constitution.

To cite one example, during the lengthy government-formation period that followed the last election, the embassy team and senior officials from Washington shuttled among the parties for months. The president and the vice president were deeply engaged. When the deal was finally sealed, there were four people in the room: Iraqi Prime Minister Nouri al-Maliki; Allawi, the leader of the Iraqiya Party; Massoud Barzani, president of the Kurdish Region; and Ambassador Jeffrey.

As that episode suggests, Iraq's leaders continue to strongly desire U.S. engagement. The United States remains the indispensable honest broker: the only party trusted by, and in daily contact with, all the leading blocs. In virtually every meeting, including when Maliki visited Obama in Washington last December, we have made clear to our Iraqi counterparts that continued U.S. support requires that they compromise across sectarian lines, respect the rule of law, and uphold their constitution.

We are clear-eyed about the fundamental challenges that Iraq still faces: finding workable ways to share power and holding all sides to the agreements they make, stamping out the violent extremists who

141

continue to launch outrageous attacks, resolving long-standing disputes about the country's internal boundaries, and ensuring that the necessary legal framework and financial arrangements are in place to allow the energy sector to further flourish.

But a little context is in order. For more than three decades, Iraq had known nothing but dictatorship, war, sanctions, and sectarian violence. In just three years, its progress toward a more normal political existence has been remarkable. Iraq still has a long way to go, but today it is less violent, more democratic, and more prosperous than at any time in recent history, and the United States remains deeply engaged there. To call Washington "absent" turns a blind eye to the facts. To call Iraq a "failed state" renders that term meaningless.

A SOLID STATE

Norman Ricklefs

Ned Parker's article reflects the new conventional wisdom among media outlets, think tanks, and large swaths of the policymaking and military communities: that Iraq is on its way to becoming a failed state, if it isn't one already. Long gone is the vision of a U.S.-aligned, democratic Iraq serving as a beacon to the rest of the Middle East. The country, pessimists such as Parker argue, suffers from terrorism, organized crime, corruption, human rights abuses, an absence of law and order, and a lack of basic services that is shameful for such an oil-rich place.

These problems are real and must be addressed. But those who decry Iraq's current state would do well to remember that the country is just now emerging from years of war, dictatorship, and sanctions. It achieved true sovereignty only in December 2011, when the last U.S. forces withdrew. For all its flaws, Iraq is actually moving in the right direction.

To begin with, the security situation has improved dramatically. Occasional coordinated terrorist attacks continue, mostly targeting Iraqi security forces and police. Only a few years ago, by contrast, the chief threat was not just irregular terrorism but also rocket and sniper attacks, kidnappings, drive-by shootings, and pitched battles in the streets. In 2006, the government did not control large parts of the capital, let alone the countryside, and elements of the security forces were unaccountable to those in power. All told, the violence that year left approximately 30,000 Iraqi civilians dead.

Since then, things have turned around. In 2007, an armed Sunni tribal movement known as the Anbar Awakening gained the upper hand over al Qaeda and, with support from U.S. and allied forces, inspired similar anti-al Qaeda groups within the Sunni community. At the same time, the U.S. troop "surge" bolstered the confidence of Iraqi government forces and anti-al Qaeda Sunnis. Meanwhile, Sunnis in Baghdad finally realized that they were losing the battle against the Shiite militias and that their past support for the insurgents had only weakened their position. These developments led to a dramatic reduction in violence and helped turn former Sunni fighters into U.S. allies.

To be sure, the most radical Sunni militias continue to attack the Iraqi government and its institutions. Terrorist attacks spiked last May, after the killing of Osama bin Laden in Pakistan, and last December, following the final withdrawal of U.S. troops. But these militias have not achieved their aim of bringing down the Iraqi government, nor have they reignited the civil war Iraq suffered in 2006 and 2007. Terrorism and criminal violence now claim on average fewer than 60 lives a week: a 90 percent reduction from 2006. What is more, most of these casualties are now caused by occasional high-profile al Qaeda attacks, not by the constant turf wars between sectarian groups that used to ravage streets and neighborhoods across the country.

Meanwhile, the Iraqi government has reined in the Shiite militias that once controlled large portions of Baghdad and the southern provinces and had fueled vicious sectarian conflicts in the mixed Sunni-Shiite provinces, especially Diyala and Nineveh. A crucial turning point came in March 2008, when Prime Minister Nouri al-Maliki sent the Iraqi army into the streets of Basra to confront militias under the command of the Shiite cleric Muqtada al-Sadr. Then, in December 2011, Maliki convinced the League of the Righteous, a prominent Shiite militia that had kidnapped and attacked U.S. forces and contractors, to renounce violence and enter into talks with his State of Law bloc.

THE BALLOT, NOT THE BULLET

Iraq's politics have also matured. Maliki's campaign in Basra demonstrated that a Shiite leader could take on Iranian-backed Shiite militias. Since then, the country's political system and civil society have mostly rewarded moderates and sidelined sectarians and radicals. In Iraq's 2010 parliamentary elections, Maliki's Dawa Party included prominent Sunni leaders on its list. Despite its history as a Shiite Islamist movement, Dawa positioned itself as centrist, and voters responded by giving the party 89 out of 325 seats in the legislature. At the same time, the secular, moderate, and mostly Sunni Iraqiya bloc, led by the former Shiite prime minister Ayad Allawi, won 91 seats. Only the Sadrists espoused a radical, anti-American message during the campaign. But they, too, moved away from organized violence and rebranded themselves as a political movement, which helped them capture 40 seats. In short, the election revealed Iraqi voters to be mature, moderate, and eager to move beyond years of bitter sectarian politics.

Since then, Iraq has suffered sporadic crises. After the election, politicians struggled to form a government for almost nine months, as Maliki and Allawi, neither of whom had won a majority, debated who had the right to form a coalition. Following a deal brokered by the United States and Iraqi Kurdish leaders, a national unity government was finally seated in December 2010. Another particularly tense moment came in December 2011, when Maliki announced that an arrest warrant had been issued for the prominent Sunni leader Tariq al-Hashimi, who occupies the mostly ceremonial post of vice president. This led to a brief boycott by the Iraqiya coalition, whose members have since returned to parliament.

Despite such hiccups, Iraq now has a functioning government, comprising representatives of all the major blocs, including Sunni ministers of finance, technology, education, and agriculture from the Iraqiya bloc. Iraqi democracy is far from perfect, but Baghdad was never going to turn into Copenhagen overnight.

Parker and others correctly note that Maliki has concentrated power in his own hands; since 2006, he has increased his direct control over the security forces and deftly played rival political forces against one another. But the prime minister's power will continue to be balanced by an increasingly independent parliament. Under the leadership of Speaker Osama al-Nujaifi, of Iraqiya, Iraq's parliament, the Council of Representatives, has begun asserting itself for the first time. The council resisted attempts by Maliki to sack the Independent High Electoral Commission in 2011 and recently extended the term of the commission despite the prime minister's opposition. Furthermore, Maliki and Nujaifi have demonstrated their ability to work together to resolve issues: they reduced the number of ministries in the government in mid-2011 and brokered an agreement between their parties over the Iraqiya boycott in January.

Iraq's economy has also made great strides, and the International Monetary Fund predicts that it will grow by more than 12 percent this year. Iraq holds foreign reserves of roughly $50 billion, its budget deficit stands at only 14 percent of GDP (down from approximately 19 percent in 2010), and inflation hovers around four percent. The value of the country's currency, the dinar, has remained mostly steady since the drop in violence in mid-2008. Meanwhile, oil revenues are set to increase as the government continues to cooperate with international companies on exporting, producing, and storing oil. Although U.S. investment in the country still lags, money has poured in from Europe, China, Iran, and Turkey. Foreign investment has risen from about $5 billion in 2006 to about $50 billion today and continues to grow roughly in line with GDP.

None of this is to deny Iraq's many problems. As Parker observes, the absence of true rule of law poses the greatest threat to the country's success. Pervasive corruption and human rights abuses, particularly in secret detention centers where prisoners are presumed guilty and denied habeas corpus, undermine Baghdad's claim to democratic legitimacy. Iraq's inefficient, Byzantine bureaucracy consistently fails to address these issues, in the process stymying growth and deterring foreign investment.

But these issues form a central part of the national discourse. Iraq's irrepressible media and its vocal political class consistently work to hold the country's leaders responsible for their deficiencies. And as security and the economy continue to improve, Iraq's civil society will be more empowered to shine light on the abuses and inefficiencies of the bureaucracy. Iraq is now an independent democracy that can provide for its own people. After decades of war and dictatorship, that is no small achievement.

PARKER REPLIES

As long as Iraq stays quiet, the Obama administration appears content with a deeply dysfunctional government in Baghdad that has tightened its grip on power and regularly violates human rights. Just as U.S. President George W. Bush once declared the war in Iraq a "mission accomplished," the Obama White House similarly boasts about its own Iraq policy, ignoring inconvenient realities in order to reap short-term political gains.

Antony Blinken tailors facts to suit his arguments instead of seriously addressing the issues my article raised. He gives the Obama administration credit for the seating of Iraq's current government in December 2010 and points to Vice President Joseph Biden's role in the process. But what Blinken fails to mention is that after making a short visit to Baghdad in January 2011, Biden did not return for another ten months. During his absence, the U.S.-brokered power-sharing deal unraveled, relations deteriorated among the country's political parties, and Prime Minister Nouri al-Maliki's military office continued operating secret detention centers, notorious for their alleged use of torture.

Iraq also failed to satisfy key conditions agreed on by its major political factions for the new unity government, including the creation of a special post for Ayad Allawi, Maliki's chief competitor. All of Iraq's security posts remain under the prime minister's control, despite stipulations during the 2010 negotiations that the main parties would apportion control of the Defense and Interior Ministries. Iraq's main Shiite, Sunni, and Kurdish factions have shown themselves unable to share power or foster mutual trust, undermining the only hope for democracy in the country. Rather than try to build a harmonious government, Maliki has driven his Sunni vice president from office on controversial terrorism charges, intimated that he might do the same to his Sunni finance minister, and attempted to fire his Sunni deputy prime minister for calling him a dictator.

Norman Ricklefs is correct to note that the Iraqi people demonstrated a preference for secular, nationalist parties in the 2010 election. But he and Blinken ignore the ugly sectarian turn that the country's politics has taken since. Maliki's state-controlled television channel popularizes stories of Shiites killed by Sunni armed groups, and the prime minister often makes speeches that pander to the Shiite community's fears. Sunni parties indulge in the same demagoguery. Ricklefs sees the decision of the League of the Righteous, a Shiite militia, to disavow violence and enter into talks with Maliki's political bloc as a positive development. But some caution is in order: Iraqi interpreters who once worked for the U.S. military report that the reformed militia continues to threaten their lives.

Celebrating Iraq's improved security is equally premature. Blinken writes that violence "has declined and remains at historic lows." But with as many as 300 people still dying each month from bombings, rocket attacks, and shootings, such declarations offer ordinary Iraqis little in the way of comfort.

Most troubling to observe is how the Maliki government has abandoned any concern for civil liberties since the 2010 election. In the intervening months, security forces have raided the offices of nongovernmental organizations, including the human rights group Where Are My Rights. Authorities beat, jailed, and even killed some civilian protesters during demonstrations last year inspired by the Arab Spring. For all the talk of Iraq's vigorous press, 65 journalists were arrested and another three were murdered in 2011.

Gone is any semblance of accountability or transparency. Several Iraqi human rights officials who uncovered abuses in the so-called black jails run by Maliki's military office have been threatened with arrest and chased from the country. Similarly, anticorruption officials have been harassed and forced from office for investigating allegations of graft on the part of both Maliki's associates and their opponents. Absent a real commitment to combating corruption, Iraq will fall victim to the resource curse that has plagued other oil-producing countries. The gains from increased energy production fill the coffers of officials in the Green Zone, but they do not benefit the majority of the Iraqi public. Despite hundreds of billions of dollars in oil revenues, 23 percent of the country lives in poverty.

Both Blinken and Ricklefs argue that Iraq, for all its flaws, has come a long way from the depths of its recent sectarian civil war. But such comparisons miss the point. Today's violence is orchestrated by the state as much as by any armed group. Fewer Iraqis cower in fear of al Qaeda, but security forces now torture detainees to extract confessions. Shiite militias are less capable of intimidation, but judges and civil servants know they must serve a political agenda or face retribution—even death. On the surface, Iraq may be calmer than it was five years ago, but it has not become a healthy state.

The West should harbor no illusions. Without impartial, transparent institutions, Iraq will fall victim to authoritarianism or civil war, if not both. The country can still be saved, but to pretend that it is marching toward democracy risks dooming it to the opposite.

When the Shiites Rise

Vali Nasr

IRAQ THE MODEL

The war in Iraq has profoundly changed the Middle East, although not in the ways that Washington had anticipated. When the U.S. government toppled Saddam Hussein in 2003, it thought regime change would help bring democracy to Iraq and then to the rest of the region. The Bush administration thought of politics as the relationship between individuals and the state, and so it failed to recognize that people in the Middle East see politics also as the balance of power among communities. Rather than viewing the fall of Saddam as an occasion to create a liberal democracy, therefore, many Iraqis viewed it as an opportunity to redress injustices in the distribution of power among the country's major communities. By liberating and empowering Iraq's Shiite majority, the Bush administration helped launch a broad Shiite revival that will upset the sectarian balance in Iraq and the Middle East for years to come.

There is no such thing as pan-Shiism, or even a unified leadership for the community, but Shiites share a coherent religious view: since splitting off from the Sunnis in the seventh century over a disagreement about who the Prophet Muhammad's legitimate successors were, they have developed a distinct conception of Islamic laws and practices. And the sheer size of their population today makes them a potentially powerful constituency. Shiites account for about 90 percent of Iranians, some 70 percent of the people

VALI NASR is a Professor at the Naval Postgraduate School, an Adjunct Senior Fellow at the Council on Foreign Relations, and the author of The Shia Revival: How Conflicts Within Islam Will Shape the Future.

living in the Persian Gulf region, and approximately 50 percent of those in the arc from Lebanon to Pakistan—some 140 million people in all. Many, long marginalized from power, are now clamoring for greater rights and more political influence. Recent events in Iraq have already mobilized the Shiites of Saudi Arabia (about 10 percent of the population); during the 2005 Saudi municipal elections, turnout in Shiite-dominated regions was twice as high as it was elsewhere. Hassan al- Saffar, the leader of the Saudi Shiites, encouraged them to vote by comparing Saudi Arabia to Iraq and implying that Saudi Shiites too stood to benefit from participating. The mantra "one man, one vote," which galvanized Shiites in Iraq, is resonating elsewhere. The Shiites of Lebanon (who amount to about 45 percent of the country's population) have touted the formula, as have the Shiites in Bahrain (who represent about 75 percent of the population there), who will cast their ballots in parliamentary elections in the fall.

Iraq's liberation has also generated new cultural, economic, and political ties among Shiite communities across the Middle East. Since 2003, hundreds of thousands of pilgrims, coming from countries ranging from Lebanon to Pakistan, have visited Najaf and other holy Shiite cities in Iraq, creating transnational networks of seminaries, mosques, and clerics that tie Iraq to every other Shiite community, including, most important, that of Iran. Pictures of Iran's supreme religious leader, Ayatollah Ali Khamenei, and the Lebanese cleric Muhammad Hussein Fadlallah (often referred to as Hezbollah's spiritual leader) are ubiquitous in Bahrain, for example, where open displays of Shiite piety have been on the rise and once-timid Shiite clerics now flaunt traditional robes and turbans. The Middle East that will emerge from the crucible of the Iraq war may not be more democratic, but it will definitely be more Shiite.

It may also be more fractious. Just as the Iraqi Shiites' rise to power has brought hope to Shiites throughout the Middle East, so has it bred anxiety among the region's Sunnis. De-Baathification, which removed significant obstacles to the Shiites' assumption of power in Iraq, is maligned as an important cause of the ongoing Sunni insurgency. The Sunni backlash has begun to spread far beyond Iraq's borders, from Syria to Pakistan, raising the specter of a broader struggle for power between the two groups that could threaten stability in the region. King Abdullah of Jordan has warned that a new "Shiite crescent" stretching from Beirut to Tehran might cut through the Sunni-dominated Middle East.

Stemming adversarial sectarian politics will require satisfying Shiite demands while placating Sunni anger and alleviating Sunni anxiety, in Iraq and throughout the region. This delicate balancing act will be central to Middle Eastern politics for the next decade. It will also redefine the region's relations with the United States. What the U.S. government sows in Iraq, it will reap in Bahrain, Lebanon, Saudi Arabia, and elsewhere in the Persian Gulf.

Yet the emerging Shiite revival need not be a source of concern for the United States, even though it has rattled some U.S. allies in the Middle East. In fact, it presents Washington with new opportunities to pursue its interests in the region. Building bridges with the region's Shiites could become the one clear achievement of Washington's tortured involvement in Iraq. Succeeding at that task, however, would mean engaging Iran, the country with the world's largest Shiite population and a growing regional power, which has a vast and intricate network of influence among the Shiites across the Middle East, most notably in Iraq. U.S.-Iranian relations today tend to center on nuclear issues and the militant rhetoric of Iran's leadership. But set against the backdrop of the war in Iraq, they also have direct implications for the political future of the Shiites and that of the Middle East itself.

THE IRANIAN CONNECTION

Since 2003, Iran has officially played a constructive role in Iraq. It was the first country in the region to send an official delegation to Baghdad for talks with the Iraqi Governing Council, in effect recognizing the authority that the United States had put in power. Iran extended financial support and export credits to Iraq and offered to help rebuild Iraq's energy and electricity infrastructure. After former Prime Minister Ibrahim al-Jaafari's Shiite-led interim government assumed office in Baghdad in April 2005, high-level Iraqi delegations visited Tehran, reached agreements over security cooperation with Iran, and negotiated a $1 billion aid package for Iraq and several trade deals, including one for the export of electricity to Iraq and another for the exchange of Iraqi crude oil for refined oil products.

Iran's unofficial influence in Iraq is even greater. In the past three years, Iran has built an impressive network of allies and clients, ranging from intelligence operatives, armed militias, and gangs to, most visibly, politicians in various Iraqi Shiite parties. Many leaders of the main Shiite parties, the Supreme Council for the Islamic Revolution in Iraq (SCIRI) and Dawa (including two leading party spokesmen, former Prime Minister Jaafari and the current prime minister, Nouri al-Maliki), spent years of exile in Iran before returning to Iraq in 2003. (SCIRI's militia, the Badr Brigades, was even trained and equipped by Iran's Revolutionary Guards.) Iran has also developed ties with Muqtada al-Sadr, who once inflamed passions with his virulent anti-Iranian rhetoric, as well as with factions of Sadr's movement, such as the Fezilat Party in Basra. The Revolutionary Guards supported Sadr's Mahdi Army in its confrontation with U.S. troops in Najaf in 2004, and since then Iran has trained Sadrist political and military cadres. Iran bankrolled Shiite parties in Iraq during the two elections, used its popular satellite television network al Aalam to whip up support for them, and helped broker deals with the Kurds. Iraqi Shiite parties attract voters by relying on vast political and social-service networks across southern Iraq that, in many cases, were created with Iranian funding and assistance.

The extent of these ties has displeased the U.S. government as much as it has caught it off-guard. Washington complains that Iran supports insurgents, criminal gangs, and militias in Iraq; it accuses Tehran of poisoning Iraqi public opinion with anti- Americanism and of arming insurgents. Washington failed to anticipate Iran's influence in Iraq largely because it has long misunderstood the complexity of the relations between the two countries, in particular the legacy of the war they fought during most of the 1980s. Much has been made of the fact, for example, that throughout that savage conflict—which claimed a million lives—Iraq's largely Shiite army resisted Iranian incursions into Iraqi territory, most notably during the siege of the Shiite city of Basra in 1982. But the war's legacy did not divide Iranian and Iraqi Shiites as U.S. planners thought; it pales before the memory of the anti-Shiite pogrom in Iraq that followed the failed uprising in 1991. Today, Iraqi Shiites worry far more about the Sunnis' domination than about Tehran's influence in Baghdad.

In addition to military and political bonds, there are numerous soft links between Iran and Iraq, forged mostly as a result of several waves of Shiite immigration. In the early 1970s, as part of his Arabization campaign, Saddam expelled tens of thousands of Iraqi Shiites of Iranian origin, who then settled in Dubai, Kuwait, Lebanon, Syria, and for the most part, Iran. Some of the Iraqi refugees who stayed in Iran have achieved prominence there as senior clerics and commanders of the Revolutionary Guards. A case in point is Ayatollah Muhammad Ali Taskhiri, who is a senior adviser to Khamenei and a doyen of the influential conservative Haqqani seminary, in Qom, where many of Iran's leading security officials and conservative clerics are educated. Taskhiri briefly returned to Najaf in 2004 to oversee the work of his Ahl al-Bayt Foundation, which has invested tens of millions of dollars in construction projects and medical facilities in southern Iraq and promotes cultural and business ties between Iran and Iraq. He is now back in Tehran, where he wields considerable power over the government's policy toward Iraq.

Throughout the 1980s and after the anti-Shiite massacres of 1991, some 100,000 Iraqi Arab Shiites also took refuge in Iran. In the dark years of the 1990s, Iran alone gave Iraqi Shiites refuge and support. Since the Iraq war, many of these refugees have returned to Iraq; they can now be found working in schools, police stations, mosques, bazaars, courts, militias, and tribal councils from Baghdad to Basra, as well as in government. The repeated shuttling of Shiites between Iran and Iraq over the years has created numerous, layered connections between the two countries' Shiite communities. As a result, the Iraqi nationalism that the U.S. government hoped would serve as a bulwark against Iran has proved porous to Shiite identity in many ways.

Ties between the two countries' religious communities are especially close. Iraqi exiles in Iran gravitated toward Iraqi ayatollahs such as Mahmoud Shahroudi (the head of Iran's judiciary), Kazem al-Haeri (a senior Sadrist ayatollah), and Muhammad Baqer al- Hakim (a SCIRI leader, killed in 2003), who oversaw the establishment of Iraqi religious organizations in Tehran and Qom. Those organizations have wielded great influence in Iran since the 1980s thanks to the role they played then in opening up the Shiites of Lebanon, who had traditionally been turned toward Najaf, to Iranian influence. Many senior clerics and graduates of the Iraqi Shiite seminaries in Iran have joined Iran's political establishment. Several judges in the Iranian judiciary, including Shahroudi, are Iraqis and are particularly close to Khamenei. And those Iraqi clerics who returned to their homeland after 2003 to take over various mosques and seminaries across southern Iraq have created an important axis of cooperation between Qom and Najaf.

So much, then, for the conventional wisdom prevailing in Washington before the war: that once Iraq was free, Najaf would rival Qom and challenge the Iranian ayatollahs. Since 2003, the two cities have cooperated. There is no visible doctrinal rift between their clerics or any exodus of dissidents from one city to the other. Grand Ayatollah Ali al-Sistani's popular Web site, www.sistani.org, is headquartered in Qom, and most of the religious taxes collected by his representatives are kept in Iran. Despite repeated entreaties from dissident voices in Iran, senior clerics in Najaf have kept scrupulously quiet about Iranian politics, deliberately avoiding upsetting the authorities in Qom and Tehran.

This nexus extends well beyond the elites. The opening of the shrine cities of Iraq has had an emotional impact on regular Iranians, especially on the more religious social classes that support the regime. Since 2003, hundreds of thousands of Iranians have visited the holy cities of Najaf and Karbala every year. This trend has reinforced the growing popularity of devotional piety in Iran. Over the past decade, many Iranian youth have taken to adulating Shiite saints, in particular the Twelfth Imam, the Shiite messiah. Many more Iranians recognize Ayatollah Sistani as their religious leader now than did before 2003, and many more now turn their religious taxes over to him. Although largely cynical about their own clerical leaders, many Iranians have embraced the revival of Shiite identity and culture in Iraq.

Business has followed religious fervor. The Iranian pilgrims who flock to the hotels and bazaars of Najaf and Karbala bring with them investments in land, construction, and tourism. Iranian goods are now ubiquitous across southern Iraq. The border town of Mehran, one of the largest points of entry for goods into Iraq, now accounts for upward of $1 billion in trade between the two countries. Such commercial ties create among Iranians, especially bazaar merchants—a traditional constituency of the conservative leadership in Tehran—a vested interest in the stability of southern Iraq.

Granted, the legacy of the Iran-Iraq War, Iraqi nationalism, and, especially, ethnic differences between Arabs and Persians have historically caused much friction between Iran and Iraq. But these factors should not be overemphasized: ethnic antagonism cannot possibly be all-important when Iraq's supreme religious leader is Iranian and Iran's chief justice is Iraqi. Although ethnicity will continue to matter to Iranian-Iraqi relations, now that Saddam has fallen and the Shiites of Iraq have risen, it will likely be overshadowed by the complex, layered connections between the two countries' Shiite communities.

These connections, moreover, are likely to be reinforced by the two communities' perception that they face a common threat from Sunnis. Nothing seems to bring Iraqi Shiites closer to Iran than the ferocity

Country	Percentage of population that is Shiite	Total population	Shiite population
Iran	90%	68.7 million	61.8 million
Pakistan	20%	165.8 million	33.2 million
Iraq	65%	26.8 million	17.4 million
India	1%	1,095.4 million	11.0 million
Azerbaijan	75%	8.0 million	6.0 million
Afghanistan	19%	31.1 million	5.9 million
Saudi Arabia	10%	27.0 million	2.7 million
Lebanon	45%	3.9 million	1.7 million
Kuwait	30%	2.4 million	730,000
Bahrain	75%	700,000	520,000
Syria	1%	18.9 million	190,000
UAE	6%	2.6 million	160,000
Qatar	16%	890,000	140,000

Notes: "Shiites" includes Twelver Shiites and excludes Alawis, Alevis, Ismailis, and Zaydis, among others. Percentages are estimated. Figures under 1 million are rounded to the nearest 10,000; figures over 1 million are rounded to the nearest 100,000.

Source: Based on data from numerous scholarly references and from governments and NGOs in both the Middle East and the West.

and persistence of the Sunni insurgency—especially at a time when their trust in Washington, which has called for disbanding Shiite militias and making greater concessions to the Sunnis, is sagging.

SUNNI SCARES

Just five years ago, Iran was still surrounded by a wall of hostile Sunni regimes: Iraq and Saudi Arabia to the west, Pakistan and Taliban-ruled Afghanistan to the east. Iranians have welcomed the collapse of the Sunni wall, and they see the rise of Shiites in the region as a safeguard against the return of aggressive Sunni-backed nationalism. They are particularly relieved by Saddam's demise, because Iraq had been a preoccupation of Iranian foreign policy for much of the five decades since the Iraqi monarchy fell to Arab nationalism in 1958. Baathist Iraq worried the shah and threatened the Islamic Republic. The Iran-Iraq War dominated the first decade of Ayatollah Ruhollah Khomeini's revolution, ravaged Iran's economy, and scarred Iranian society.

If there is an Iranian grand strategy in Iraq today, it is to ensure that Iraq does not reemerge as a threat and that the anti-Iranian Arab nationalism championed by Sunnis does not regain primacy. Iranian President Mahmoud Ahmadinejad and many leaders of the Revolutionary Guards, all veterans of the Iran-Iraq War, see the pacification of Iraq as the fulfillment of a strategic objective they missed during that conflict. Iranians also believe that a Shiite-run Iraq would be a source of security; they take it as an axiom that Shiite countries do not go to war with one another.

All this is small consolation for the Sunnis in the region, who remember the consequences of Iran's ideological aspirations in the 1980s—and now worry about its new regional ambitions. A quarter century ago, Tehran supported Shiite parties, militias, and insurgencies in Bahrain, Iraq, Kuwait, Lebanon, Pakistan, and Saudi Arabia. The Iranian Revolution combined Shiite identity with radical anti-Westernism, as reflected in the hostage crisis of 1979, the 1983 bombing of the U.S. Marine barracks in Beirut, and Tehran's continued support for international terrorism. In the end, the Iranian Revolution fell short of its goals, and except for in Lebanon, the Shiite resurgence that it inspired came to naught.

Some say the Islamic Republic is now a tired dictatorship. Others, however, worry about the resurgence of Iran's regional ambitions, fueled this time not by ideology but by nationalism. Tehran sees itself as a regional power and the center of a Persian and Shiite zone of influence stretching from Mesopotamia to Central Asia. Freed from the menace of the Taliban in Afghanistan and of Saddam in Iraq, Iran is riding the crest of the wave of Shiite revival, aggressively pursuing nuclear power and demanding international recognition of its interests.

Leaders in Tehran who want to create a greater zone of Iranian influence—something akin to Russia's concept of "the near abroad"— view Tehran's activities in southern Iraq as a manifestation of Iran's great-power status. Yet none of them holds on to Khomeini's dream of ruling over Iraq's Shiites. Rather, Tehran's goal in southern Iraq is to exert the type of economic, cultural, and political influence it has wielded in western Afghanistan since the 1990s. Although Tehran clearly expects to play a major role in Iraq, it may not aim—or be able—to turn the country into another Islamic republic.

Predictably, Iran's growing prominence is complicating relations between sectarian groups in the region. Sunni governments have used Tehran's ambitions as an excuse to resist both the demands of their own Shiite populations and Washington's calls for political reform. Since 2003, Sunni leaders in Egypt, Jordan, and Saudi Arabia have repeatedly blamed Iran for the chaos in Iraq and warned that Iran would wield considerable influence in the region if Iraqi Shiites came to hold the reins of power in Baghdad. The Egyptian president, Hosni Mubarak, sounded the alarm last April: "Shiites are mostly always loyal to Iran and not the countries where they live." Such partly self-serving rhetoric allows Sunni leaders to divert attention away from their own responsibility for Iraq's troubles: Egypt, Jordan, and Saudi Arabia have so far supplied the bulk of Abu Musab al-Zarqawi's army of suicide bombers. It also provides them with a subterfuge to resist U.S. calls for domestic political reform. If bringing democracy to the Middle East means empowering Shiites and strengthening Iran, they argue, Washington would be well advised to stick to Sunni dictatorships.

The Sunnis' public-relations offensive worries the Iranian leadership. Despite its growing clout, Tehran needs its neighbors' support and the goodwill of "the Arab street" to resist international pressure over its nuclear program. So far, Tehran has avoided sectarian posturing and further antagonizing Sunnis; instead, it has tried to generate support in the region by escalating tensions with the United States and Israel. Iranian leaders have routinely blamed sectarian violence in Iraq, including the bombing of the Askariya shrine, in Samarra, in February, on "agents of Zionism" intent on dividing Muslims. Meanwhile, Tehran aggressively pursues nuclear power both to confirm Iran's regional status and to minimize Washington's ability to stand in its way.

A MEETING OF MINDS

Iran's aspirations leave Washington and Tehran in a complicated, testy face-off. After all, Iran has benefited greatly from U.S.-led regime changes in Kabul and Baghdad. But Washington could hamper the consolidation of Tehran's influence in both Afghanistan and Iraq, and the U.S. military's presence in the region threatens the Islamic Republic. In Iraq especially, the two governments' short-term goals seem to be at odds: whereas Washington wants out of the mess, Tehran is not unhappy to see U.S. forces mired there.

So far, Tehran has favored a policy of controlled chaos in Iraq, as a way to keep the U.S. government bogged down and so dampen its enthusiasm for seeking regime change in Iran. This strategy makes the current situation in Iraq very different from that in Afghanistan after the fall of the Taliban in late 2001, when Iran worked with the United States to cobble together the government of Hamid Karzai. Tehran cooperated with Washington at the time largely because it needed to: its Persian-speaking and Shiite clients in Afghanistan made up only a minority of the population and were in no position to protect Iran's interests. Tehran's calculus in the aftermath of the Iraq war has been different. Not only do Iran's immediate interests not align with those of the United States, but Tehran's position in Iraq is stronger than it was in Afghanistan thanks to the majority status of Shiites in Iraq. Seeing the Bush doctrine proved wrong in Iraq would be an indirect way for Iran's leaders to discredit Washington's calls for regime change in Tehran. Their recent willingness to escalate tensions with Washington over Iran's nuclear activities suggests that they believe they have largely succeeded in this goal; Iran is now stronger relative to the United States than it was on the eve of the Iraq war.

And yet, in the longer term, U.S. and Iranian interests in Iraq may well converge. Both Washington and Tehran want lasting stability there: Washington, because it wants a reason to bail out; Tehran, because stability in its backyard would secure its position at home and its influence throughout the region. Iran has much to fear from a civil war in Iraq. The fighting could polarize the region and suck in Tehran, as well as spill over into the Arab, Baluchi, and Kurdish regions of Iran, where ethnic tensions have been rising. As former Iranian Deputy Foreign Minister Abbas Maleki has put it, chaos in Iraq "does not help Iranian national interest. If your neighbor's house is on fire, it means your home is also in danger." Clearly wary, Tehran has braced itself for greater troubles by appointing a majority of its provincial governors from the ranks of its security officials and Revolutionary Guard commanders.

Two groups within Iran could help convince the Iranian leadership that cooperation with Washington is in its interest. The first are Iraqi refugees, who act as a lobby for Iraqi Shiite interests in Tehran. They have encouraged Iran to pursue talks with the United States over Iraq, partly because they view Washington and Tehran as the twin pillars of their power in Iraq. The escalation of tensions between the two governments would not serve the interests of Iraqi Shiites, and that lobby does not want to see Iraq become hostage to the international standoff over Iran's nuclear program. The second important constituency is made up of the many Iranians who are greatly concerned about the sanctity of Iraq's shrine cities. Every major bombing in Najaf and Karbala so far has claimed Iranian lives. The Iranian public expects Tehran to ensure the security of those cities; its influence has already provided Khamenei with a pretext for publicly endorsing direct talks with Washington over Iraq.

Still, Iran will actively seek stability in Iraq only when it no longer benefits from controlled chaos there, that is, when it no longer feels threatened by the United States' presence. Iran's

long-term interests in Iraq are not inherently at odds with those of
the United States; it is current U.S. policy toward Iran that has set
the countries' respective Iraq policies on a collision course. Thus a
key challenge for Washington in Iraq is to recalibrate its overall
stance toward Iran and engage Tehran in helping to address Iraq's
most pressing problems.

SETTING THE STAGE

The most important issue facing Iraq in the coming months will be
the constitutional negotiations, particularly regarding the questions of federalism and how oil revenues will be distributed. It was
only after the U.S. ambassador to Iraq, Zalmay Khalilzad, persuaded the Shiites and the Kurds to agree to change the constitution that the Sunnis participated in the referendum to ratify it in
late 2005. Since then, Washington has hoped for a deal that would
bring moderate Sunnis into the political process and thus weaken
the Sunni insurgency. But the prospects of such a deal are uncertain. The Shiites, the Sunnis, and the Kurds are unlikely to see the
wisdom of compromise without outside pressure, and the U.S.
government no longer has the political capital to force concessions
or satisfy the demands of one party without risking alienating another. It is the weakening of the United States' position in Iraq that
makes it necessary—more so now than in 2003—for Washington
to reach out to Iraq's neighbors. If the constitutional negotiations
fail, the Sunnis could abandon the political process.

Even if the Sunnis participate, bargaining with the Shiites
may become more complicated, especially given signs of increasing turmoil in southern Iraq. Over the past three years, the Shiites have both participated politically and resisted the Sunni
insurgency's provocations, largely because they have believed
that backing U.S. policy would serve their interests. But if they
were to conclude that Washington is now more eager to buy the
Sunnis' cooperation than to reward them for their steadfastness,
the Shiites might turn their backs on the political process. Such
an upset could spark a Shiite uprising. The Shiites would not

even need to pick up arms to pressure the United States; by virtue of their numbers alone, they can change the country's political balance. In January 2004, Sistani rallied hundreds of thousands of Shiites for five days of demonstrations against U.S. plans to base the first post-Saddam elections on a caucus system. Earlier this year, he called the crowds to the streets again to protest the Askariya shrine bombing—and to ensure that the U.S. government understood the extent of Shiite power.

Given its clout among the Shiites in southern Iraq, Tehran could help maintain order there while the constitutional negotiations were under way. Iran could ensure that the growing rivalry among Shiite factions such as SCIRI and Sadr's troops did not spin out of control, destabilize southern Iraq, and erode government authority in Baghdad. Keeping the Shiites together and maintaining calm in the south is of singular importance to the United States, and Iranian cooperation is crucial to achieving that goal. Iran's cooperation would help address Iraq's security and reconstruction needs, as well as buttress the central government in Baghdad.

But securing such cooperation would require the United States to address broader issues in its relationship with Iran. Tehran will end its military and financial support to Shiite militias and criminal gangs in southern Iraq only if it receives broad security guarantees from Washington. The current situation in Iraq is similar to that in Afghanistan in 2001 in the way it seems to entangle U.S. and Iranian interests—only it is more complicated and the stakes are higher. After the fall of the Taliban in Afghanistan, the United States and Iran worked closely together to bring the Northern Alliance and its Shiite component into the mainstream political process. Washington and Tehran negotiated intensely on the sidelines of the Bonn conference on the future of Afghanistan, striking deals that helped ensure the early successes of the Karzai regime. The Bonn process promised to open a new chapter in the history of U.S.- Iranian relations. But at the time, Washington had little interest in further engaging a regime it believed it would soon overthrow. It missed an important opportunity then.

Iraq's troubles today offer Washington and Tehran a second great chance not only to normalize their relations, but also to set the stage for managing future tensions between Shiites and Sunnis. The Shiites' rise to power in Iraq sets an example for Shiites elsewhere in the Middle East, and as the model is adopted or tested it is likely to exacerbate Shiite-Sunni tensions. Better for Washington to engage Tehran now, over Iraq, than wait for the problem to have spread through the region. Although Washington and Tehran are unlikely to resolve their major differences, especially their dispute over Iran's nuclear program, anytime soon, they could agree on some critical steps in Iraq: for example, improving security in southern Iraq, disbanding the Shiite militias, and convincing the Shiite parties to compromise.

But if Washington and Tehran are unable to find common ground—and the constitutional negotiations fail—the consequences would be dire. At best, Iraq would go into convulsions; at worst, it would descend into full-fledged civil war. And if Iraq were to collapse, its fate would most likely be decided by a regional war. Iran, Turkey, and Iraq's Arab neighbors would likely enter the fray to protect their interests and scramble for the scraps of Iraq. The major front would be essentially the same as that during the Iran-Iraq War, only two hundred miles further to the west: it would follow the line, running through Baghdad, that separates the predominantly Shiite regions of Iraq from the predominantly Sunni ones. Iran and the countries that supported it in the 1980s would likely back the Shiites; the countries that supported Iraq would likely back the Sunnis.

Iraq is sometimes compared to Vietnam in the early 1970s or Yugoslavia in the late 1980s, but a more relevant—and more sobering—precedent may be British India in 1947. There was no civil war in India, no organized militias, no centrally orchestrated ethnic cleansing, no battle lines, and no conflict over territory. Yet millions of people died or became refugees. British India's professional army was sliced along communa 13bc l lines as the country was partitioned into Hindu-majority and Muslim-majority regions. Unable to either

163

bridge the widening chasm between both groups or control the violence, the British colonial administrators were forced to beat a hasty
retreat. As in Iraq today, the problem in India then lay with a minority that believed in its own manifest destiny to rule and demanded, in
exchange for embracing the political process, concessions from an un-
yielding majority. The pervasive sectarian violence and ethnic cleansing plaguing Iraq today are ominous reminders of what happened in
India some 60 years ago. They may also be a worse omen: if the situation in Iraq deteriorates further, the whole Middle East would be at
risk of a sectarian conflict between Shiites and Sunnis.

Iraqi Sunnistan?

Why Separatism Could Rip the Country Apart—Again

Emma Sky and Harith al-Qarawee

It's not easy being a prominent Sunni in Iraq these days. This past December, Iraqi Prime Minister Nouri al-Maliki ordered the arrest of several bodyguards of Rafi al- Issawi, the minister of finance and one of the most influential and respected Sunni leaders in Iraq. In response, tens of thousands of Sunnis took to the streets of Anbar, Mosul, and other predominantly Sunni cities, demanding the end of what they consider government persecution. Issawi has accused Maliki of targeting him as part of a systematic campaign against Sunni leaders, which includes the 2011 indictment of Vice President Tariq al-Hashimi, a Sunni, on terrorism charges. This is not the first time that Maliki has gone after Issawi, either. In 2010, during tense negotiations over the makeup of the government, Maliki accused Issawi of leading a terrorist group—a claim that the U.S. military investigated and found baseless. Not coincidentally, this most recent incident occurred days after President Jalal Talabani, always a dependable moderator in Iraqi politics, was incapacitated by a stroke.

The scale of the ongoing demonstrations reveals the widespread sense of alienation that Sunnis feel in the new Iraq. Prior to 2003,

EMMA SKY is a senior fellow at Yale University's Jackson Institute for Global Affairs. From 2007 to 2010, she was the political adviser to Ray Odierno (then the commanding general of U.S. Forces in Iraq).

HARITH AL-QARAWEE is an Iraqi political scientist and the author of Imagining the Nation: Nationalism, Sectarianism and Socio-political Conflict in Iraq.

Sunnis rarely identified as members of a religious sect and instead called themselves Iraqi or Arab nationalists. It was the country's Shia population that claimed to be victims, on account of their persecution by Saddam Hussein.

Today, the roles are reversed. Shia Islamists consolidated power in Baghdad after the toppling of Saddam's regime, and some—particularly those who were exiled during Baathist rule—now view all Sunnis with suspicion. In turn, many Sunnis take issue with the new political system, which was largely shaped by Shia and Kurdish parties. Today, the Sunni population is mobilizing against the status quo and making sect-specific demands, such as the release of Sunni detainees, an end to the torture of Sunni suspects, and humane treatment of Sunni women in jails. Moreover, demonstrators are calling for the overthrow of the regime, using slogans made popular during the Arab Spring.

Meanwhile, Kurdish leaders identify Maliki as the main problem facing Iraq, and some delegations of Kurds and Shia have travelled to Issawi's native province of Anbar to express their own distrust of the regime. The top Iraqi Shia cleric, Grand Ayatollah Sistani, has voiced disappointment with Maliki's government and has called for it to respond to the concerns of the protestors. Muqtada al-Sadr, the leader of Iraq's most authentic grassroots Shia movement, the Sadrist Trend, has accused Maliki of provoking the current discontent. Although fear of Maliki's creeping authoritarianism is pushing his rivals together, growing sectarian tensions may yet rip Iraq apart.

As with other protests in the Arab world, which were initially driven by legitimate local grievances, there is a risk that the current movement will become increasingly sectarian. At political events, some Iraqi Sunni clerics use conciliatory language and emphasize Iraqi fraternity. Others, however, speak passionately about the suffering of the Sunni community at the hands of Maliki's Shia administration and condemn his ties with Iran.

Since 2008, when Maliki led a harsh crackdown on the Mahdi Army, a Shia militia, the prime minister has tried to present himself as a nationalist leader seeking to unify his country and evenly enforce the rule of law. The rise of Maliki and the popularity he gained with Shia, however, reveal the flaws of Iraq's new political system, which made state institutions fiefdoms of patronage for sectarian political parties rather than channels for delivering public services. Maliki tried to earn legitimacy beyond just the Shia community, in particular seeking the support of Sunni voters. His confrontation with Massoud Barzani, the president of the semi-independent Iraqi Kurdistan region, over security issues along the disputed border was primarily a move to win the support of the Sunni population there, which is resentful of Kurdish encroachment.

But Maliki has squandered his ability to appeal to the country's other sects and communities because of his paranoia and ideological bias as a leader of Dawa, the Shia Islamist party. He blames external interference for the current tensions, exploiting images of divisive symbols such as flags of the Saddam era, the Free Syrian Army, and Kurdistan, as well as photos of Turkish Prime Minister Recep Tayyip Erdogan. And Maliki's record—his targeting of Sunni politicians, his selective use of law, his influence over the judiciary to ensure rulings in his favor, and his close ties with Iran—confirms that he is prepared to use all means necessary to consolidate power.

Maliki could cling to power by presenting himself as the defender of the Shia in an increasingly tumultuous environment, turning his fear of a regional sectarian conflict into a self-fulfilling prophecy. Al-Qaeda attacks in Iraq are on the rise, provoked by discontent with Maliki and inspired by the Syrian civil war next door. So far this month, al-Qaeda has killed Shia pilgrims in Karbala, a Sunni lawmaker in Anbar, and Kurds in Kirkuk. Meanwhile, other leaders are struggling to remain relevant. The credibility of Sunni government officials is declining, due to their inability to prevent discrimination against their constituents while participating in a system that brings them personal benefits. In the Shia camp, Sadr is moving to the center, positioning himself as a nationalist leader. If Sadr is able to create an alliance with anti-Maliki Sunnis and Kurds—presenting a credible and unifying alternative government—sectarianism could be curbed. However, Maliki might be provoked by such a challenge and clamp down on his rivals even more aggressively.

Politics in Iraq and the surrounding region are increasingly sectarian. Inspired by the rebellion in Syria and supported by the Sunni leaders of Turkey, Saudi Arabia, and Qatar, Iraq's Sunnis may seek greater autonomy from the Shia-dominated central government in years to come. This need not be the case: in the 2010 national elections, most Sunnis voted for the Iraqiya electoral list, a coalition that defined itself as nonsectarian and was led by a secular Shia politician. But, given the sectarian turn of Iraqi politics, Sunni leaders seem likely to run on one list with a platform built around Sunni grievances in the 2014 national elections. In addition, more hardline Sunni leaders may emerge if the current politicians prove unable to achieve meaningful gains for their communities. Sunni leaders may also, if they manage to overcome their internal divisions, propose an independent Sunni region, similar to the one enjoyed by the Kurds. This would mark the end of Iraqi nationalism and put the survival of the state in question.

Maliki's efforts to destroy his rivals have drawn him closer to Shia Iran, which has in turn affected regional power dynamics. To counter Iran's influence, Turkey is now posing as the defender not only of Iraq's Sunnis but also of its Kurds, even though Turkey has long feared Kurdish nationalism within its own borders. Saudi Arabia, despite its usual counterrevolutionary attitude, is supporting the rebels in Syria in hopes of replacing the Shia-Alawite regime with a Sunni government and undoing the pro-Shia axis that now runs through Iran, Iraq, Syria, and Lebanon.

It is up to Iraq's politicians, then, to overcome their differences and construct a national platform that addresses the country's challenges. Any such settlement will require making concessions regarding regional autonomy, internal border disputes, the management and distribution of oil profits, and Baghdad's foreign policy orientation. Unfortunately, given mutual distrust, the personalization of disputes, and the upcoming electoral season, such compromises do not seem likely—particularly if Maliki insists on remaining in power indefinitely.

The American public is no doubt fatigued by the recent decades of involvement in the country and the region. But to avoid disaster, the United States urgently needs to review its Iraq policy. Washington needs to show the Iraqi people that its intent is not to divide Iraq and keep it weak—even if that appears to have been a main outcome of the U.S. intervention. U.S. President Barack Obama succeeded in keeping his campaign promise of withdrawing U.S. forces from Iraq. In its second term, the Obama administration should stop supporting a status quo that is driving Iraq toward both authoritarianism and fragmentation. The United States should make clear that it neither condones nor supports the prime minister's consolidation of power and blatant use of the Iraqi Security Forces—which the United States helped train and equip—to crack down on political opposition. Washington should make its aid to Maliki—or any other Iraqi leader—conditional on his behaving within democratic norms.

In addition, Washington should support Iraqi Shia's attempts to select a new prime minister and should help facilitate a pact among the country's elites in order to turn Iraq into a buffer rather than a battlefield state in the volatile region. U.S. engagement in the Middle East should seek to restrain external actors from interfering in Iraq and waging a proxy war there. Washington needs to contain Iran, but should make clear that it is not aligned with Sunnis in a regional sectarian war against Shia. This will require pushing back on Iranian influence in Iraq and simultaneously putting greater pressure on Sunni allies in the region to respect and protect their Shia populations. The United States has invested too much in Iraq to simply ignore these warning signs. Washington should use its diplomatic clout to help prevent further bloodshed.

Collateral Damage in Iraq

The Rise of ISIS and the Fall of al Qaeda

Barak Mendelsohn

O n its lightning-fast advance through Iraq, the radical jihadi group the Islamic State of Iraq and al-Sham (ISIS)
has captured Mosul, Iraq's second-largest city; Tikrit,
Saddam Hussain's birth city; and many other towns along the way.
Now, with help from former Baathists and Sunni tribal forces, the
group is making its way toward Baghdad. ISIS' astonishing success
could be a harbinger of a tectonic shift within the jihadi movement.
Namely, ISIS could supplant al Qaeda as the movement's leader.

This showdown has been several years in the making. The friction between the two groups goes back years. But the relationship
did not reach a breaking point until April 2013, when Abu Bakr
al-Baghdadi, the leader of ISIS, expanded his group into Syria and
attempted to subordinate the local al Qaeda branch, Jabhat al-
Nusra (JN), to his own authority. JN rejected Baghdadi's leadership, and Ayman al-Zawahiri, al Qaeda's chief, tried to calm the
dispute by announcing that JN would remain responsible for jihad
in the Syrian arena and ISIS would keep to Iraq. ISIS refused to
accept Zawahiri's decision and continued its expansion into Syria.

BARAK MENDELSOHN is an Associate Professor of political science at
Haverford College and a Senior Fellow at the Foreign Policy Research Institute
(FPRI). Follow him on Twitter @BarakMendelsohn.

Along the way, it trampled other Syrian rebel groups, including radical Islamists. Soon, ISIS' overreach provoked a backlash, and opposing rebel groups mounted a counteroffensive. For its part, JN eventually sided with the anti-ISIS forces. By February 2014, the rift between ISIS and the Syrian opposition had led Zawahiri to disown the group.

The differences between ISIS, on the one side, and al Qaeda and JN, on the other, are not merely about power and control of the jihadi movement. As important as these aspects are, the groups have serious differences when it comes to strategy, tactics, and Islamic authority. They differ on issues such as the implementation of harsh Islamist laws, the killing of Shia civilians, and the right of one group to impose its authority over all others. The groups don't disagree about the legitimacy of all of these things, but al Qaeda is more patient and ISIS is generally more radical and uncompromising. For that reason, its traipse through Iraq represents a serious organizational, strategic, and ideological blow to al Qaeda.

ISIS' display of power will likely strengthen its hand over al Qaeda in Syria and beyond. First, the military successes brought the group substantial spoils: ISIS looted bank deposits worth close to $500 million, captured large quantities of military equipment, and liberated hundreds of fighters from prisons in territory now under its control. All of that will prove very useful in Iraq and in Syria. As money and manpower breed success, success will breed more success. ISIS' popularity will likely rise among radicals, and that will translate into more funding and volunteers for the group. ISIS could rapidly mobilize those forces along the vanishing border between Iraq and Syria, which it now increasingly controls, and launch even more ambitious campaigns while it fends off attacks in Syria.

Second, beyond raising ISIS' profile, the terrorist group's march through Iraq also diminishes al Qaeda's. Al Qaeda's greatest achievement was the 9/11 attacks, but that was 13 years ago. Many of today's jihadis were young children at that time. Moreover, the attack on the United States was only supposed to be a means to an end: the establishment of an Islamic caliphate in the heart of the Middle East. Al Qaeda franchises did manage to gain (and then lose) some territory in Yemen, Somalia, and northern Mali. But these territories are smaller in size and significance than what al Qaeda wanted—and what ISIS controls today. Although al Qaeda may have started the march toward the reestablishment of the Caliphate, it is ISIS that seems to be realizing it.

Third, success breeds legitimacy. For the past year, al Qaeda's main tactic against ISIS has been to try to delegitimize the movement. And, until now, al Qaeda's strategy had been moderately successful. Popular jihadi scholars, such as Abu Muhammad al-Maqdisi and Abu Qatada al-Filistini, released messages of support for al Qaeda and strongly denounced ISIS—which turned some would-be adherents away from the upstart. ISIS was able to muddle through the delegitimization campaign by hanging on to the support of some young and popular jihadi scholars. And, even before the surprise in Iraq, the trend in the jihadi movement had been toward the decentralization of religious authority; social media offers a platform for nearly any charismatic jihadi to gain a following. At the same time, moreover, young jihadis have increasingly come to view the old guard—often identified with al Qaeda—as disconnected from reality. They give more respect to warriors than to religious scholars. All that plays to ISIS' favor, especially now that it has real victories under its belt. It can use those as evidence that it has been right all along and that its ways are truthful. Zawahiri's criticisms, delivered from his hiding place in Pakistan, are weak in comparison.

Fourth, symbolism works to ISIS' advantage. In the past, al Qaeda, Syrian rebel groups, and numerous jihadi scholars criticized Baghdadi's claim that ISIS represents a genuine Islamic Emirate— with rights that surpass any privileges a jihadi organization may claim—by arguing that control over territory is essential for the creation of Islamic Emirate. Now, ISIS holds territory larger than many countries. Similarly, although Baghdadi has been criticized for using the title Emir of the Believers, which is reserved for the

Caliph, his organization's recent accomplishments make the title seem more appropriate. Further, it is lost on few radical Islamists that Baghdadi's forces—merely 5,000 men—defeated 90,000 soldiers on a march toward Baghdad, the seat of the Abbasid Caliphate for 500 years.

War is, of course, unpredictable, and ISIS' good omens could evaporate if it doesn't hold on to its gains. Unfortunately for al Qaeda (and Iraqis and Syrians), that seems unlikely to happen. ISIS' march is the result of a well-thought-out plan that was a long time in the making. The crumbling Iraqi military is ill equipped to quickly reverse ISIS' progress, and the United States appears unwilling to step in, at least in a dramatic way.

Al Qaeda knows that. And so, despite the animosity between the two groups, it seems to be bound to congratulate its rival for its victories. It might offer advice, but it can't go against ISIS. It will be expected to offer support or at the least cheer for its rival, not stick a knife in its back. To al Qaeda's further disadvantage, disagreements over methods and authority are increasingly less salient. Al Qaeda's appeal relative to ISIS' is greater when questions of how to run a territory populated by Sunni Muslims who do not subscribe to the Salafi-jihadi radical interpretation of Islam take center stage. When the front stabilizes and the intensity of the fight subsides, such questions will return and the inherent weakness of ISIS will resurface. ISIS is an extremely capable force, but its battle achievements do not make it any more appealing as a government. To succeed in the competition with ISIS, al Qaeda could try to outdo it in some way—through advances against the Assad regime, quality operations in the Arabian Peninsula and in North Africa, and attacks in the West. Still, given the weakening of al Qaeda's central command, the limitations of its franchises, and this most recent blow to its reputation, its ability to recover is far from certain.

Kurds to the Rescue

How to Get the Kurdish Regional Goverment to Take on ISIS

Dov Friedman and Cale Salih

The Islamic State of Iraq and al-Sham (ISIS) now occupies a territory the size of Jordan, stretching from the edge of Aleppo to the outskirts of Baghdad. From there, it poses a grave threat to regional and U.S. security interests. Yet those who seek to stop it have few options. ISIS easily trounced the Iraqi security forces, which outnumbered the jihadist group 100-1. And it could likely do the same to the Iranian Revolutionary Guards that have trickled over the border to bolster the Iraqi forces; Iran's elite fighters are simply spread too thin across Syria and Iraq. Meanwhile, the United States seems unwilling to send U.S. troops back into the fray at all.

Enter the Kurdistan Regional Government (KRG) and its skilled (and intact) *peshmerga* forces. The Kurds field the only proper army left in Iraq, and, for that reason, the United States and Iran will each attempt to draw the Kurds into the conflict. Yesterday, during a meeting in Tehran between Kurdish Prime Minister Nechirvan Barzani and Ali Shamkhani, the secretary of Iran's Supreme National Security Council, Iranian officials reportedly asked the Kurds to join the fight against ISIS. U.S. officials apparently

DOV FRIEDMAN is a graduate student at Yale University's Jackson Institute for Global Affairs. Follow him on twitter @DovSFriedman.

CALE SALIH is a researcher specializing in Iraq, Syria, and Lebanon. Follow her on twitter @callysally.

hope that the Kurds will step in as well. Indeed, if Washington wants to quell ISIS, the *peshmerga* are its best bet.

But will the United States and Iran get what they want? Some think so. Among oil executives and seasoned Iraq analysts, for example, some believe that the Kurds can be moved by the prospect of oil revenues and budgetary guarantees alone. The KRG has piped nearly three million barrels of oil to Ceyhan, Turkey, but it has struggled to sell its product on the world market—not least due to Baghdad's interference. Should the Kurds cease to meet resistance on oil sales, the thinking goes, they will be more inclined to support the United States and Iran against ISIS.

And there are good reasons for the KRG to work for ISIS' demise. In the past, Sunni jihadists have targeted the KRG, and one week before ISIS took control of Mosul, it attacked a Patriotic Union of Kurdistan (PUK) office in Diyala, killing 18 people. ISIS is unpredictable and it could, in the near future, pose legitimate security risks to the Kurdish region. For a Kurdish government that has cultivated a reputation for providing security, ISIS attacks would be a massive blow. Moreover, although ISIS has trained its attention on Baghdad for the time being, military conflict with the Kurds could flare up in several places. ISIS is fighting sporadically with the *peshmerga* in northern Diyala, which the Kurds want to control because of its proximity to the Kurdish-majority city of Khanaqin. In Kirkuk, too, the line between the *peshmerga* and ISIS is dangerously taught. The Kurds control most of the province. Sunni insurgents, however, control the southern parts, including Hawija—the site of deadly violence between Sunni protestors and the Iraqi government last year. According to a Kurdish source, the region now shares a 1000-kilometer (620-mile) border with insurgents.

But those expecting Kurdish enthusiasm for a fight are likely to be disappointed. They underestimate the current strength of the Kurdish position and the continued sting of decades past, when the Kurds gave their support to the West and got nothing in return. In fact, the Kurds have drawn their battle lines north of

Mosul, across the south of Kirkuk province, and through northern Diyala province. So long as ISIS respects that line, Kurdistan—which banks on its reputation as a stable, private-sector friendly outpost in a region fraught by sectarian turmoil—would have very little reason to invite war. After all, the Kurds have spent a decade cultivating this reputation. The KRG has fashioned a strong military with broad public support, and the government has deftly managed relations with Turkey and Iran. While Iraqis in the rest of the country live in perpetual conflict, Kurds in Erbil, the Kurdish capital, live with perpetual construction. Sustaining this success, which is largely built on oil wealth, depends on maintaining security.

History is an issue too. Simply mention the year 1975 to any Kurd, and, within moments, one will hear of U.S. Secretary of State Henry Kissinger's "betrayal"—the Algiers Agreement, which temporarily ended the conflict between Iraq and Iran. The agreement left the Iraqi Kurds, who had supported the Iranian Shah, to suffer at the hands of the Baathists. The treachery is seared into Kurdistan's collective memory as a reminder of the dangers of leaving oneself to the mercy of the established powers.

For the Kurds, 1975 is not the only problem. In the early days of the Iraq War, U.S. special forces and Kurdish *peshmerga* fought together against the Ansar al-Islam insurgency. The Kurds believed they had proved themselves stalwart U.S. allies, but then Paul Bremer, leader of the coalition provisional government in Iraq, sought to disarm them. After sweeping through Kirkuk in 2003, heavy U.S. pressure forced the Kurds to pull back—a moment the KRG leadership rued for years before reclaiming the revered city late last week. In addition, the Obama administration's general disengagement from Iraq has baffled Kurdish leaders and left them with scant reason to fight on the United States' behalf

The United States isn't the only player the Kurds mistrust. They are no fans of the Iraqi army—with which they may have to coordinate—either. In the city of Jalawla, Iraqi artillery recently fired on Kurdish forces instead of ISIS insurgents. Six *peshmerga* died, embittering Kurdish citizens and fueling resentment of the Iraqi army.

Yet, Kurdish troops remain the best hope for those who want to stop ISIS in Iraq, and the Obama administration will likely attempt to persuade them to join the offensive—or at least to provide substantial logistical and intelligence support to the Iraqi army. There are several things the administration must do if it desires Kurdish participation. First, it must end any talk of bolstering Iraqi Prime Minister Nuri al-Maliki. Maliki is a divisive brute whom Iran supports to the hilt. U.S. intimations of continued support for him will only rally the Sunni opposition, which would be radioactive for the KRG. Instead, Washington (and Tehran) should insist that Maliki put a stop to inflammatory rhetoric among members of his party and state media. Such rhetoric—allusions to an ISIS-Kurdish conspiracy, in particular—is rapidly alienating the Kurdish public.

Second, the United States must offer something concrete to the Kurds now. One option is to ease the way for the sale of Kurdish oil. The KRG has repeatedly sent tankers filled with oil into international waters seeking buyers and come back empty-handed. The United States must quietly drop its objections to Kurdish independent oil sales and facilitate the finding of willing buyers. It should then continue to support the development of an independent revenue stream to the KRG.

Third, the United States must arm the *peshmerga*. Mere months ago, U.S. President Barack Obama agreed to provide Maliki with yet another shipment of advanced U.S. weapons, and ISIS fighters now brandish many American-made arms. Such is the cost of Washington's unflinching support for the Iraqi security forces. If the West seeks Kurdish help in rooting out ISIS, it must show similar commitment by arming the Kurdish military and providing support through air strikes as necessary.

Finally, the United States must commit to the KRG that it will support Kurdish claims to the disputed territories it recovered last week. For the United States to promise Kirkuk to the KRG would be foolish—a promise that the Kurds know the United States can't fulfill. But a promise to tacitly accept Kurdish claims is another matter. This reassurance, too, must be delivered silently, as the final status of Kirkuk is an Arab- Kurdish-Turkmen issue to solve. No one would question the KRG's skepticism at such a promise, although bold U.S. support in other ways might just convince the KRG of U.S. fidelity.

It is precisely the Kurdish belief—a fair one—that the United States has been an unreliable partner that makes the cost of Kurdish participation so high today. The Kurds maintain the dominant position in Iraq: unified, militarily superior, and little affected by internecine Arab strife. That could all change against an unpredictable foe like ISIS. But seeking out the fight is another matter entirely. To prevail upon the KRG to undertake the task, the United States must effectively bind itself to the Kurdish cause. Even then, the KRG may sit out this fight until its immediate interests are at stake, and no one could fault it. As is so often the case, it is history that presents the greatest obstacle to the fight against ISIS.

The Fallacy of Iranian Leverage

Why the Turmoil in Iraq Will Weaken the Islamic Republic

Dalia Dassa Kaye

In the breathless coverage of the bloody advance of the Islamic State of Iraq and al- Sham (ISIS) through Iraq, some news analysis has suggested that the ISIS victories could actually boost Iranian leverage in the region. According to this view, since the Shia government of Prime Minister Nouri al-Maliki is increasingly relying on Iranian support to hold off ISIS expansion, Iran's influence in the region could rise and its hand in the nuclear negotiations with the West could consequently strengthen.

The West's nuclear talks with Iran are nearing a critical July 20 deadline for a final deal, so it isn't surprising to hear speculation about how ISIS' victories will affect the negotiations. Israeli leaders, for example, have expressed concerns that the United States may try to push through a less than optimal deal as it is tempted to work with Iran to confront a common adversary in Iraq. And other neighbors, such as Saudi Arabia, share similar concerns about diminished American influence and increased Iranian regional power. But this way of thinking misreads the fallout of the Iraq crisis and its relationship to the nuclear negotiations.

DALIA DASSA KAYE is a senior political scientist and the director of the Center for Middle East Public Policy at the nonprofit, nonpartisan RAND Corporation.

For one, Iran has its own reasons to counter ISIS, for which the United States will not need to pay a price. ISIS is a threat to Iran because of its anti-Shia ideology and because it is menacing a friendly ally in Baghdad, which has ensured that Iraq poses no strategic threat to Iran. ISIS gains also put in jeopardy Iran's broader strategic alliances with Syria and Hezbollah by capturing territory through which Iran typically sends Hezbollah armaments.

To be sure, Sunni extremists' efforts to stir sectarian strife through brutal atrocities against Iraqi Shia will no doubt make the Iraqi government and the country's majority Shia population more amenable to overt Iranian assistance and influence in the country. But they were already fairly amenable to begin with: Maliki has already demonstrated as much by pursuing anti-Sunni sectarian policies that helped fuel support for ISIS to begin with. And his long-standing ties to Iran are likewise no secret; many attribute his resistance to a continued U.S. military presence in Iraq after 2011 to Iranian influence. To think that any outcome in Iraq would leave Iran without considerable influence is foolish.

But with ISIS gains threatening to lead to a de facto partition of the country, Iranian influence might actually be more contained than it has been in recent years. It would likely be limited to the Shia south—a setback for an Iranian government that would like all of Iraq to be under its sway. And the price for maintaining such influence could be higher: the rump Iraqi state may need more assistance from Iran at a time when it is is already stretched thin.

If ISIS continues to secure key strategic oil, gas, and power facilities in Iraq, it might be able to cut off electricity and energy supplies to Baghdad. Iran could fill some of this gap to support the Shia-led government in Iraq, but Iranian oil and gas products are heavily subsidized and in short supply, so doing so would create a further drain on the Iranian economy at a time when Iran's precarious domestic situation created the pressures that brought it to the negotiating table with the West to begin with.

Militarily, an Iraqi state surrounded by ISIS will face challenges securing its own borders. Iran could help, but the Iranian Quds Force is already busy keeping Assad afloat in Syria. Iran will no doubt find the manpower and resources—or shift them—to deal with this more urgent threat on its border, but it could suffer the consequences in Syria. Eventually, the financial gains and momentum from the take-over of major Iraqi cities (and banks) will flow back across the border to ISIS forces in Syria. To keep Assad in power, Iran would thus have to invest more blood and treasure, not less. But it isn't clear that the country could do that while fighting in Iraq and absent a nuclear deal and its accompanying sanctions relief.

Finally, the specter of a wider regional sectarian war stemming from the ISIS offensive is a losing proposition for Iran. After all, Shia are outnumbered in the region and Iran cannot ultimately exert broader regional influence without some support from Sunni Muslim populations. Iran used to enjoy some such backing because of its hostility to the West and Israel and its support for Hezbol-lah's confrontations against Israel, but that has been in rapid de-cline since the onset of the Arab uprisings and Iran's support in suppressing the Sunni opposition in Syria. For that reason, Iranian President Hassan Rouhani has been particularly interested in tamping down sectarian tensions with key neighbors, such as Saudi Arabia, which would be essential for ultimately resolving the proxy war in Syria. A new proxy war in Iraq pitting Sunni-backed forces against the Shia government and militia forces supported by Iran will make such reconciliation efforts impossible.

In other words, rather than helping Iran in the nuclear negotia-tions, Iran's battle against the ISIS could actually hurt it. The broader strategic dynamics were already working against Iran, and the situation in Iraq has only made that more true.

There is a tendency in the United States to believe that a loss for the West must be a gain for Iran. But, in Iraq, both sides are losing in the face of a common foe. This coincidence of interest could increase Iran's incentives to strike a nuclear deal so that it can get the economic relief it desperately needs to be able to address both its domestic pressures as well as its growing regional chal-lenges. If the ISIS crisis and its associated costs for Iran boosts the prospects for a nuclear deal that can definitively prevent Iran from weaponizing its nuclear program for the foreseeable future, it would be an unexpected positive spillover from an otherwise miserable regional situation.

Who Lost Iraq?

And How to Get It Back

Emma Sky

Republicans and Democrats each share some of the blame for the situation in Iraq—the former for the way in which the United States entered the country and the latter for the way in which it left. It was only between 2007 and 2009 that the United States had a coherent strategy in Iraq, matched with the right leadership and the necessary resources. The current turmoil dates back to just after that period, to 2010, after Iraq's second post-Saddam national election.

At that time, some senior officials argued that the United States should uphold the constitutionally mandated right of the winning bloc, Iraqiya, headed by Ayad Allawi, to have the first go at trying to form a government. They maintained that the United States should actively help broker an agreement among Iraqi elites to form the new government and warned of the already apparent autocratic tendencies of Nouri al- Maliki, the incumbent prime minister.

Other officials argued that Maliki, despite his narrow electoral defeat, was the only conceivable Shia leader who could hold the position. He was also, they said, a friend of the United States who would agree to allow the United States to maintain a small contingent of forces in Iraq after 2011, when the existing agreement between the two countries expired. In the end, it was Iran that

EMMA SKY is a senior fellow at Yale University's Jackson Institute for Global Affairs. From 2007 to 2010, she was the political adviser to Ray Odierno (then the commanding general of U.S. Forces in Iraq).

stepped in and, by pressuring the Sadrists to support Maliki, secured him a second premiership. The price Iran extracted from Maliki was his support for the removal of all U.S. forces.

Since 2010, Maliki has consolidated his power by targeting his political rivals, subverting the judiciary and independent government commissions, reneging on his promises to the Sunni tribal leaders who had helped him fight al Qaeda, and politicizing the security forces that the United States invested so much in training. He also mishandled the yearlong protests against his government that erupted in Sunni areas at the end of 2012, following the souring of relations between him and Rafi al-Issawi, the highly respected minister of finance. His forces attacked protesters in Hawija, killing 50. Then, in December 2013, he sent troops into western Anbar to attack the desert camps of a Sunni radical group, the Islamic State of Iraq and al-Sham (ISIS). Following the death of the Iraqi general leading the operation, Maliki ordered his troops into the cities of Anbar province to close down all protest sites.

Maliki's moves seemed to be tactical successes in that they strengthened his regime. But they have been revealed to be strategic disasters, since they provoked a backlash that weakened the state. With the ISIS takeover of cities in the provinces of Anbar, Ninewa, and Salah al-Din, that reality has been made clear. Iraqi security forces, which outnumber ISIS by around a hundred to one, deserted and fled their positions as ISIS advanced; soldiers' morale was low and a number of senior officers owed their positions to bribes and political affiliation rather than to competence. Sunni tribes, which previously had turned against the forerunner of ISIS, al Qaeda in Iraq, have this time either fled, remained neutral, or backed the militants. Given their sense of disenfranchisement, they do not trust Maliki's government to provide for them or to protect them. Some have concluded that ISIS is the lesser of two evils. Sunni clerics in Iraq, along with regional media, are now referring to the Sunni "revolt" against Maliki's government.

ISIS' victories are a result of internal divides, rising sectarianism, state failure, and geopolitical competition in two neighboring countries. In one of his recent speeches, Abu Bakr al-Baghdadi, the leader of ISIS, called on Sunni Muslims to join his organization to fight the Shia and establish a caliphate, which would remove the borders between Muslim lands that were demarcated by colonial powers. "Give up corrupt nationalism," he urged, "and join the nation of Islam."

But it is not the borders that are the root of the problems of these countries. It is the political leadership, which has failed to develop inclusive and robust states. Grievances against the governments of Maliki and Bashar al-Assad in Syria have created the environment in which ISIS can prosper. And, ironically, although the ISIS has railed against national divisions, the tensions between its international jihadist agenda and the nationalist agendas of most Sunni groups will inevitably create friction and infighting. For now, though, ISIS will find plenty of Sunnis willing to join the fray.

Meanwhile, facing the shock caused by the collapse of the Iraqi army in Mosul, Shia have turned to Ayatollah Ali al-Sistani for guidance. Sistani issued a fatwa calling on Iraqis to join the security forces in the fight against ISIS. Despite Sistani's statement that the fatwa was intended for Sunni and Shia civilians alike, Shia militias are using it as an occasion for sectarian mobilization.

In the ongoing turmoil, the Kurds have taken the contested city of Kirkuk and see independence in their sights. U.S. forces invested considerable time and resources in mediating between the different parties in these disputed territories. Without such a neutral third party, the likelihood of Arab-Kurdish conflict is increasing, with ISIS gaining the opportunity to present itself as the protector of the Sunnis against Iranian- backed Shia but also against what they perceive as Kurdish expansionism.

So what can and should the United States do? It is positive that the United States no longer views the violence in Iraq as separate from the bloodshed in Syria and Lebanon. The region has become one battlefield—and U.S. policy must reflect that. It was the 1979 Iranian Revolution that set off the modern-day struggle between

Iran and the Sunni powers. And it was the 2003 war in Iraq that led to sectarianization of regional politics. Then it was the 2011 U.S. departure from Iraq that left the impression in the region that Iran had defeated the United States. The United States needs to pursue policies that lessen sectarian tensions and support moderates. The majority of those living in Iraq and Syria yearn to live in peace with just, effective, and transparent governments. The choice before them cannot simply be Iranian-backed exclusionary regimes or al Qaeda–linked affiliates.

Although the United States and Iran face a common threat in ISIS, the United States should cooperate with Iran only if it leads to major reform of Iraq's political system so as to overcome sectarian divisions. If not, the specter of a perceived alignment between the United States and Iran could worsen sectarianism and push more Sunnis toward ISIS.

The main political tensions in Iraq today are between Maliki's drive to centralize power, the Kurds' desire to maximize their autonomy, and the increasing Sunni awareness of themselves as a distinct community. The fall of Mosul and events that followed are indications that these tensions have come to a head and that it is time for Maliki to admit his failures and open the way for a more competent Shia leader to start a new approach. Although Maliki did head the winning bloc in the most recent elections, those opposed to him have enough votes to replace him if they can agree on an alternative. Iraq's political elites, in particular the Shia parties, need to select a new prime minister who is acceptable to them and to other communities, and is supported by Iran and Turkey as well as the United States.

In his June 19 statement, U.S. President Barack Obama said, "Iraqi leaders must rise above their differences and come together around a political plan for Iraq's future. Shia, Sunni, Kurds—all Iraqis—must have confidence that they can advance their interests and aspirations through the political process rather than through violence." Obama is right to pressure Iraqi politicians to form a new government, rather than insisting that they support Maliki.

He correctly recognized that any military options would be effective only if they were in support of an overall political strategy that a new broad-based government agreed to. The United States has a key role to play in helping broker a new deal among the elites that creates a better balance among Iraq's communities. A new broad-based Iraqi government will need to win back the support of Sunnis against ISIS—and the Obama administration should be prepared to respond positively to requests for assistance to do so.

Maliki Isn't the Problem

The Roots of Sectarianism in Iraq

Kevin Russell and Nicholas Sambanis

T he news that the Islamic State of Iraq and al-Sham (ISIS) had taken control of Mosul on its way toward Baghdad caught Americans by surprise.

It shouldn't have. More than a third of all ethnic civil wars restart within five years. And about a third of all post-conflict power-sharing agreements fail within the same time frame. For example, in Angola, concessions to increase representation through multiparty elections led to a new bout of war in 1991. In Afghanistan, the losing side remobilized in 1992, 1996, and 2001. And in Sri Lanka, a 2002 ceasefire collapsed in 2006.

In other words, today's reignition of the 2006–07 Iraqi civil war fits a well-established pattern. And that pattern has several implications for U.S. strategy in the region.

PEACE IN PIECES

Peace after an ethnic civil war is so tenuous because violence reifies ethnic identities and post–civil war politics is inevitably cast along ethnic lines. This creates a dilemma. To cultivate peace, citizens

KEVIN RUSSELL is a Ph.D. Candidate in Political Science at Yale University. He was an Iraq policy analyst for the Department of Defense from 2006-08 and State Department Governance Specialist in 2008-09.

NICHOLAS SAMBANIS is Professor of Political Science at Yale University.

must learn to identify with their nation more than their ethnic group. But leaders often stand in their way. Since officials do not trust that nationalism will fully replace parochialism, they are reluctant to give up the sectarian basis of their political power in favor of the unknown. And so they play to ethnic tensions to shore up their bases.

Iraq illustrates the dilemma. U.S. observers and officials increasingly demonize Iraqi Prime Minister Nouri al-Maliki, who they say is to blame for sectarian conflict. But he is a symptom more than a cause.

At first, Maliki enjoyed the support of some Sunni leaders who appreciated his decisive moves against Shia militias in early 2008. But their trust in him was never complete; they wanted to wait and see how he would treat the Sunnis who had fought al Qaeda in Iraq and had participated in local and national elections in 2009 and 2010. Needless to say, Sunnis were soon disappointed as Maliki personalized his rule, politicized the security services, and resorted to the old sectarian politics.

At the same time, though, to attribute all the blame to Maliki is to assume that sectarian conflict is due to a few bad leaders. Before Maliki, Sunnis had held power in Iraq since the British mandate. These authoritarian regimes had put down all forms of civil society, but as groups, the Shia and Kurdish populations suffered under the Sunni dominated hierarchy. From Maliki's perspective, every Sunni leader thus constituted a threat to his rule; there was no reason to believe in their commitment to national institutions. The apparent Sunni acquiescence to ISIS' latest push only confirmed Maliki's fears. Although other Shia leaders would be glad to take his place, they would face the same political logic.

All this means that the plan U.S. President Barack Obama laid out last Thursday—the United States will share intelligence with Iraq and help the country coordinate a plan to turn back ISIS in return for Maliki promising to share power with Sunni leaders—won't work. The sectarian dilemma will persist even if ISIS is defeated, and any feints at sharing power are likely to be short-lived.

It is up to Iraqi politicians to overcome the sectarian dilemma. But leaders' loyalties can only gradually change from their sect to their nation. Politicians must follow the constitution and limit their power to create public expectations about the rule of law. Citizens might then vote on performance rather than sect, but that process can take decades and is hard to get started.

Third-party interventions can help move things along by providing monitoring for both sides and helping keep spoilers at bay. Yet interventions' very success often brings mounting pressure to restore full sovereignty to the nation. Third parties are asked to leave before new patterns of behavior are entrenched, which creates a power vacuum.

That is certainly what happened in Iraq. The United States fought hard for five years to open a window for impartial state building. But the window started closing in 2008 when the United States committed to withdrawal by 2011.

In general, only impartial interventions—the ones that provide assistance at a scale large enough to be effective and small enough to be tolerated by the national authorities—can last long enough to succeed. And that also holds true in Iraq. At this point, another round of intense American involvement would be hard for Iraqis (and Americans) to stomach. But, at the same time, the current level of U.S. commitment to Iraq is perceived to be too low to keep Maliki—and any successor—from falling back on sectarianism.

LESS IS MORE

So what can the United States do? The country might still want to help Iraq defeat ISIS, since it deems that doing so is in its interests. But it should intervene in a way that improves the chances for longer-term stability. Rather than treat Iraq's request for support as an opportunity to solicit non-credible political promises, for example, the United States would have to reengage. It would have to commit to doing much less than last time, precisely so that it can commit to doing it for much longer.

Doing less would mean promising not to return conventional U.S. troops to Iraqi territory. This is the primary red line for both the American and Iraqi publics. On the other hand, committing to staying involved for longer would allow for military and diplomatic strategies that offer Iraqi leaders incentives to establish bases of power that are not purely dependent on sect. Since the U.S. diplomat Paul Bremer administered the Iraqi Coalition Provisional Authority in 2003–04, five governments have been formed around the hope that sectarian leaders could share power. They all failed. The United States needs to commit for as long as it takes for Iraqi leaders to make successful appeals to constituents outside their sect—at least several more elections.

What might such a commitment entail?

Militarily, Obama's offer of intelligence assistance, advisors, and possible airstrikes would have to be considered the start of a real partnership in training, civil-military administration, and ongoing operations. A stronger military-to-military relationship would make it harder for a Shia prime minister to politicize the armed forces and, on the flip side, make the military a less threatening platform for a possible Sunni coup.

The fight with ISIS is a regional conflict that requires a regional solution. It took a Central America–wide peace effort to end El Salvador's civil war and a similar collective approach to end Cambodia's genocidal war. Ultimately, the same is needed in Iraq (and Syria), but "friends" who could shepherd a peace process are in short supply. Iran and some Arab states have waged a proxy war in Syria. To gain at least tacit consent for U.S. reengagement in Iraq, it will be necessary to appeal to their shared interest (along with Russia and Turkey) in denying ISIS a state. More optimistically, the ISIS crisis might provide a diplomatic opening to limit the flow of arms and funds across Syrian and Iraqi borders.

Within Iraq, convening Kurdish, Shia, and Sunni leaders was always a tiresome exercise of brinkmanship and crisis management for U.S. diplomats, made even harder by the ticking clock of the withdrawal. The United States should now play the long game and work toward non-sectarian nationalism. That means moving away from a focus on divvying up ministries and toward one on jobs and political participation for the Sunni lower and middle classes, including within the tribes outside of Baghdad.

At this point, the most important measure of success for any U.S. strategy in Iraq is whether it prevents a regional war. Iraq is the region's lynchpin due to its geographical location and its relationships with other countries in the area. Accordingly, the United States should make Iraq the central pillar of a regional strategy based on the "lighter, longer" principles of no ground troops and no disengagement. Targeting extremists and shoring up the moderates will be difficult, but Iraq is not Syria, where the United States cannot even identify the interests of a fractured array of fighters. Americans fought to establish relationships in Iraq. Now it is time to take them further and help Iraqi leaders develop new constituencies that are not defined by sectarian identity. If the United States doesn't play this limited but long-term role, the sectarian cycle will repeat and engulf the region.

The sectarian power-sharing strategy is not working, but even that is probably better than doing nothing. It at least gives the United States a foothold in Iraq to ensure that ISIS does not acquire its own state. But the strategy is shortsighted at best. In his 2009 "New Beginning" speech in Cairo, Obama said that "America has a dual responsibility: to help Iraqis forge a better future—and to leave Iraq to the Iraqis." This meant withdrawing ground troops while supporting Iraq as a military and economic partner. Obama has only lived up to part of his commitment to Iraq. It is not too late to live up to the other.

Securing al-Sham

Syria and the Violence in Iraq

Andrew J. Tabler

U prooting the Islamic State of Iraq and al Sham (ISIS) from the swath of territory it now holds between Aleppo and Baghdad will take a lot more than airstrikes or a change of government in Iraq. Although the 2003 war in Iraq might have led to the formation of the jihadi group, the chaos in Syria provided it the space to metastasize. To prevent ISIS—and other such organizations—from building a permanent safe haven in Iraq and Syria, then, Washington must help settle Syria by supporting Sunni tribes and other moderate opposition groups there.

FRACTURED FRONT

Over the last week, the Obama administration has focused its attention on pushing Iraqi Prime Minister Nouri al-Maliki (or whoever might replace him) to be more inclusive of the country's Sunni Arabs, who make up around 20 percent of the population. Washington is right to do so. ISIS and the other groups fighting alongside it rely on this disenchanted community for support. Without Sunni backing, ISIS would crumble and Iraq could stabilize. To help that process along, the United States could launch airstrikes against ISIS camps in the country.

Sunni Arabs are an even larger part of the equation in Syria, where they represent between 65 and 70 percent of the population

ANDREW J. TABLER is senior fellow at the Washington Institute for Near East Policy and author of In the Lion's Den: An Eyewitness Account of Washington's Battle with Syria. Follow him on Twitter @andrewtabler.

and make up the backbone of the opposition to the Alawite Assad regime. Western mediators have urged Assad to negotiate with Alawites, Shia, and Sunnis. But he has refused, preferring instead to have himself "re-elected" to a third term as president and to make vague promises of dialogue with the opposition groups that succumb to the regime's siege-and-starve tactics.

Assad might seem like he is in control, but his troops rarely tangle with ISIS, preferring instead to take on the more moderate factions. In fact, his regime has only been able to go on the offensive in western Syria with help from Hezbollah, Iraqi Shia militias, and Iran's Quds force. When their support disappears, so, too, will Assad's luck. For example, when Iraqi Shia militiamen were recently recalled from the Lebanese-Syrian frontier to fight ISIS in Iraq, Syrian opposition forces quickly reappeared, retook part of the area, and continued to stage hit-and-run attacks. In other words, Assad and the rebels are at a stalemate and, unless the West and its Arab allies try something new, the conflict will persist.

BORDERLANDS

The best way to permanently uproot ISIS is to follow the example of Jordan. In recent years, Jordan has relied on a two-part strategy to deal with the Syrian crisis: control the border with Syria and monitor and work with the Syrian opposition to keep radical rebel groups out of the country's southern reaches, along the border with Jordan. The U.S. intelligence community, which has a close relationship with Jordan, has reportedly participated in this effort.

Moderate groups continue to hold their own in southern Syria, but, as in other areas of the country, they still rely on coordination with more radical groups to fight the Assad regime. To prevent those radical groups from spilling into Jordan, Amman closed one of its border crossings to refugees and reopened it further east, in uncontested territory. It also worked with Western intelligence agencies to increase covert support for moderate groups in southern Syria. As a result, ISIS has yet to take root there.

For Turkey to strengthen its own border with northern Syria, it would have to follow Jordan's example. So far, though, Ankara has been reluctant to get as strict about people, money, and weapons crossing its frontier into and out of Syria. There is considerable risk that militants could retaliate against Turkey if it decided to clamp down, but surely the Syrians roaming its territory already present such a risk. To help Turkey make the right call, the United States could promise to use drones or airstrikes to help Turkey secure the border.

After closing the borders between Syria and Jordan and Syria and Turkey, it will be time to address the now-gaping border between Syria and Iraq. The best way to do that is by working with tribes in the area and with selective drone strikes. Sunni tribal confederations such as the Baggara, Dulaim, Jabbour, N'eim, Qugaidat, Shammar, and Tai'e extend into Syria and Iraq—and some even reach into Qatar, Saudi Arabia, and the United Arab Emirates. These tribes could be made into a bulwark against ISIS and other jihadists in Syria and Iraq. According to some reports, ISIS has worked to win over their rank and file by offering basic services. For those that don't accept such carrots, the group has used harsh sticks, such as beheadings and crucifixions. Its pull among the tribal population worries local tribal leaders, who see their influence slipping.

Arab intelligence agencies can play on these fears by supplying tribal leaders with lethal and nonlethal assistance. The United States is not in a good position to lead this effort, since it has no boots on the ground and lacks the qualitative intelligence. However, Washington should coordinate closely with Arab Gulf countries in supporting tribes against militant groups, using air power to aid their fight against ISIS.

Another natural bulwark against ISIS and other such groups is Syria's Kurdish population in northeast Syria. To stave off the militant threat, the Kurds united two years ago under the banner of the Kurdish Supreme Committee. The group includes the radical Democratic Union Party of Syria, which is the Syrian offshoot of the Kurdistan Workers' Party, and the more moderate Kurdistan National Council, an alliance of 15 Kurdish political parties. Despite tensions among its members, the alliance has battled jihadists for the better part of two years. And like their Arab counterparts, the Kurds are also organized into broad tribal confederations that reach across the border into Iraq and Turkey.

Sealing off Syria's external borders—and its internal one with the Kurdish region—would help contain jihadist groups and interdict ISIS suicide operators coming to Iraq while the United States works with the Iraqi government to win over moderate Sunnis and, possibly, launches drone strikes against ISIS positions. This could be bolstered through the creation of a U.S. Joint Special Operations Task Force to coordinate cross- border operations. Meanwhile, allying with the Arab tribes on both sides of the border will undermine ISIS support in its key Sunni Arab demographic. This could result in a foreign policy twofer, helping address both the current situation in Iraq and Syria and the broader jihadist threat over the long term.

SYRIAN SOLUTION

With ISIS hemmed in, the crisis in Iraq would be far easier to manage through airstrikes and diplomacy.

The world could then turn to the war in Syria. The top-down diplomatic efforts to resolve the crisis are going nowhere. According to Samantha Power, U.S. representative to the United Nations, more Syrian civilians died from Assad's barrel bombs during this year's failed peace talks in Geneva than during any other period in the Syrian war. And that onslaught continues to this day. The best way to keep the regime from dropping barrel bombs, as well as chlorine gas and other indiscriminate weapons, would be to shoot down its aircraft.

Providing vetted armed groups with antiaircraft weapons would help the opposition secure its territory. It would also empower moderates by making them key to defending against Assad's onslaught. Although antiaircraft guns would not take care of the regime's weapon of choice—artillery—civilians would at least have less reason to flee to Turkey and Jordan, which are already overwhelmed with refugees and fear spillover violence. The United States could provide the opposition active intelligence to facilitate such operations.

Now the question is how to channel antiaircraft and other heavy weapons so that they don't fall into radicals' hands. Much has been made of the bickering and petty rivalries within the Syrian National Coalition (SNC) and the thousand or so armed groups fighting against the Assad regime. The divisions are partly a reflection of Syria's extremely diverse Sunni population—from the urbane Sunnis representing the traditional elites, who long collaborated with the regime, to the tribal Sunnis of eastern Syria and Dera, who cooperated with the regime at arm's length, to the conservative Sunnis of northwestern Syria, who have long fought Alawites and the Assad regime. ISIS and other militant groups, such as the al Qaeda affiliate Jabhat al-Nusra, are primarily entrenched within the tribal and conservative Sunni populations.

The Supreme Military Council (SMC), an umbrella organization that Arab and Western intelligence helped set up in late 2012 as the armed wing of the SNC, was meant to unify rebels' supply chains, encourage moderates to unite, and empower the SNC on the ground. Unfortunately, it hasn't worked, which coalition leaders blame on a lack of outside support. The problem with the SMC is that, like the SNC, it is beset with petty rivalries and has at times been infiltrated by radical Salafis. For that reason, it would be unwise to use the SMC, at least as it exists now, to channel antiaircraft weapons to moderate rebels.

The other major conduit supporting the rebels has been individual groups vetted by Western and Arab intelligence agencies, including the Syrian Revolutionary Front and Harakat Hazm, which have been given American-made antitank missiles. Such vetted groups stand wholly apart from their more radical counterparts, but their lack of resources or political agenda has hobbled them. The SMC leadership, moreover, has criticized Western efforts to supply some groups with weapons as creating warlordism among the moderate Syrian opposition.

But given the threat that jihadist groups pose in Syria, selective arming seems like the least bad option. And antiaircraft weapons would come with strings attached. In the short term, the regional intelligence agencies that are advising moderate groups inside Syria would be best placed to carry out joint antiaircraft operations until the moderate Syrian opposition can stand on its own. Over the longer term, the SMC should be reconstituted as a clear anti-radical force with more tribal leaders and leaders from vetted groups. As was the clear during the SMC's initial formation, Arab and Western intelligence agencies are best placed carry out the task. A new SMC could be the channel for other heavy weapons as well and the conduit for setting up governments in opposition areas coordinated with the SNC and other groups in exile.

Eventually, as the SMC's capabilities increase, the group could fill vacuums in areas where ISIS and other jihadi groups give way. Eventually, the SMC would fully train its sights on the Assad regime. Assad, in turn, would come to appreciate that his military solution to the Syria conflict is doomed to fail and that he needs to return to the negotiating table.

PAYING UP

For the second time in less than a year, U.S. President Barack Obama is considering military strikes in the Middle East. Targeted air, missile, and drone attacks could degrade ISIS' capabilities and should be used carefully. But they will not fix the region's problems—especially the ongoing war between the Tigris and Euphrates rivers.

The United States must start to address those problems by increasing covert support for border security operations and for the Syrian opposition. To do so, it can tap the $5 billion Counterterrorism Partnerships Fund that Obama recently outlined in a speech at West Point. This fund aims to expand the training and equipping of foreign militaries, bolster allied counterterrorism capabilities, and support efforts to counter violence extremism and terrorist ideology.

Yet Syrians cannot unite around groups armed in the shadows. A much more comprehensive and overt training and equipping program, as recently introduced in the National Defense Authorization Act, would help the United States build up moderate forces in Syria that could effectively combat Assad and deescalate the crisis. Although it is still unclear which moderate Sunni oppositionists will be part of any final negotiated settlement, it is clear is that ISIS and other radicals can't be included.

www.ingramcontent.com/pod-product-compliance
Lightning Source LLC
Chambersburg PA
CBHW072223270326
41930CB00010B/1973